Kazakh Vocabulary:
A Kazakh Language Guide

Ruslan Nabiyev

Contents

List of Kazakh letters

Order	Kazakh Cyrillic alphabet	Kazakh Latin alphabet	IPA
01	A a	A a	/ɑ/
02	Ә ә	Ä ä	/æ/
03	Б б	B b	/b/
04	В в	V v	/v/
05	Г г	G g	/g/
06	Ғ ғ	Ğ ğ	/ʁ/
07	Д д	D d	/d/
08	E e	E e	/i̯ə/
09	Ё ё	Yo yo	/jo/
10	Ж ж	J j	/ʒ/
11	З з	Z z	/z/
12	И и	Ï ï	/əj/, /əj/
13	Й й	Y y	/j/
14	К к	K k	/k/
15	Қ қ	Q q	/q/
16	Л л	L l	/l/
17	М м	M m	/m/
18	Н н	N n	/n/
19	Ң ң	Ñ ñ	/ŋ/
20	О о	O o	/u̯ʊ/
21	Ө ө	Ö ö	/yʉ/
22	П п	P p	/p/
23	Р р	R r	/r/
24	С с	S s	/s/
25	Т т	T t	/t/
26	У у	W w	/w/, /ʊw/, /ʉw/
27	Ұ ұ	U u	/ʊ/
28	Ү ү	Ü ü	/ʉ/
29	Ф ф	F f	/f/
30	Х х	X x	/x, χ/
31	һ h	H h	/h/

32	Ц ц	C c	/t͡s/
33	Ч ч	Ç ç	/t͡ɕ/, /t͡ʃ/
34	Ш ш	Ş ş	/ʃ/
35	Щ щ	Şş şş	/ɕ:/
36	Ъ ъ	"	
37	Ы ы	I ı	/ə/
38	I i	İ i	/ə/
39	Ь ь	'	
40	Э э	É é	/e/
41	Ю ю	Yu yu	/jʉw/, /jʊw/
42	Я я	Ya ya	/jɑ/

1) Measurements
1) Өлшем бірліктері
1) Ölşem birlikteri

acre
акр
akr

---

area
аудан
audan

---

case
қорап
qorap

---

centimeter
сантиметр
santimetr

---

cup
кесе
kese

---

dash
шай қасықтың 1/8 бөлігі
şay qasıqtıñ 1/8 böligi

---

degree

градус

gradus

depth

тереңдік

tereñdik

digit

бірлік

birlik

dozen

он екі

on eki

foot

фут

fut

gallon

галлон

gallon

gram

грамм

gramm

height

биіктік

biïktik

huge

алып

alip

inch

дюйм

diuyim

kilometer

километр

kilometr

length

ұзындық

uzındıq

liter

литр

litr

little

аз

az

measure

өлшем

ölşem

meter

метр

metr

mile

миля

mïlya

minute

минут

mïnut

miniature

кішігірім

kişigirim

ounce

унция

untziya

perimeter

периметр

perimetr

pint

пинта

pïnta

pound

фунт

funt

quart

кварта

kvarta

ruler
сызғыш
sızğış

---

scale
масштаб
masştab

---

small
кішкентай
kişkentay

---

tablespoon
ас қасық
as qasıq

---

teaspoon
шай қасық
şay qasıq

---

ton
тонна
tonna

---

volume
көлем
kölem

---

weigh
өлшеу
ölşeu

---

weight

салмақ

salmaq

---

width

ен

en

---

yard

ярд

yard

Time
Уақыт

Waqıt

What time is it?

Сағат қанша болды?

Sağat qanşa #/boldbold#ı?

It's 1:00 AM/PM

Сағат 1:00 болды

Sağat 1:00 boldı

It's 2:00 AM/PM

Сағат 2:00 болды

Sağat 2:00 boldı

It's 3:00 AM/PM

Сағат 3:00 болды

Sağat 3:00 boldı

It's 4:00 AM/PM

Сағат 4:00 болды

Sağat 4:00 boldi

It's 5:00 AM/PM

Сағат 5:00 болды

Sağat 5:00 boldi

It's 6:00 AM/PM

Сағат 6:00 болды

Sağat 6:00 boldi

It's 7:00 AM/PM

Сағат 7:00 болды

Sağat 7:00 boldi

It's 8:00 AM/PM

Сағат 8:00 болды

Sağat 8:00 boldi

It's 9:00 AM/PM

Сағат 9:00 болды

Sağat 9:00 boldi

It's 10:00 AM/PM

Сағат 10:00 болды

Sağat 10:00 boldi

It's 11:00 AM/PM

Сағат 11:00 болды

Sağat 11:00 boldi

It's 12:00 AM/PM
Сағат 12:00 болды
Sağat 12:00 boldi

---

in the morning
таңғы
tañğı

---

in the afternoon
түскі
tüski

---

in the evening
кешкі
keşki

---

at night
түнде
tünde

---

afternoon
түстен кейін
tüsten keyin

---

annual
жылдық
jıldıq

---

calendar
күнтізбе
küntizbe

---

daytime

күндіз

kündiz

decade

он жылдық

on jıldıq

evening

кеш

keş

hour

сағат

sağat

midnight

түн ортасы

tün ortası

minute

минут

mïnut

morning

таң

tañ

month

ай

ay

night

түн

tün

---

nighttime

түнгі уақыт

tüngi waqıt

---

noon

түс

tüs

---

now

қазір

qazir

---

o'clock

сағат

sağat

---

past

өткен шақ

ötken şaq

---

present

осы шақ

osı şaq

---

second

секунд

sekund

---

sunrise

таңның атуы

tañnıñ atuı

sunset

күннің батуы

künniñ batuı

today

бүгін

bügin

tonight

бүгін кешке

bügin keşke

tomorrow

ертең

erteñ

watch

сағат

sağat

week

апта

apta

year

жыл

jıl

yesterday

кеше

keşe

Months of the Year
Жылдың айлары
Jıldıñ ayları

January

Қаңтар

Qañtar

February

Ақпан

Aqpan

March

Наурыз

Naurız

April

Сәуір

Säuir

May

Мамыр

Mamır

June

Маусым

Mausım

July
Шілде
Şilde

August
Тамыз
Tamız

September
Қыркүйек
Qırküyek

October
Қазан
Qazan

November
Қараша
Qaraşa

December
Желтоқсан
Jeltoqsan

Days of the Week
Аптаның күндері
Aptanıñ künderi

Monday
Дүйсенбі
Düysenbi

Tuesday

Сейсенбі

Seysenbi

Wednesday

Сәрсенбі

Särsenbi

Thursday

Бейсенбі

Beysenbi

Friday

Жұма

Juma

Saturday

Сенбі

Senbi

Sunday

Жексенбі

Jeksenbi

Seasons
Жыл мезгілдері

Jıl mezgilderi

winter

кыс

kıs

---

spring

көктем

köktem

---

summer

жаз

jaz

---

fall/autumn

күз

küz

Numbers
Сандар
Sandar

One(1)

Бір(1)

Bir(1)

Two(2)

Екі(2)

Eki(2)

Three(3)

Үш(3)

Üş(3)

Four(4)

Төрт(4)

Tört(4)

Five(5)

Бес(5)

Bes(5)

Six(6)

Алты(6)

Altı(6)

Seven(7)

Жеті(7)

Jeti(7)

Eight(8)

Сегіз(8)

Segiz(8)

Nine(9)

Тоғыз(9)

Toğız(9)

Ten(10)

Он(10)

On(10)

Eleven(11)

Он бір(11)

On bir(11)

Twelve(12)

Он екі(12)

On eki(12)

Twenty(20)

Жиырма(20)

Jiırma(20)

Fifty(50)

Елу(50)

Elu(50)

Hundred(100)

Жүз(100)

Jüz(100)

Thousand(1000)

Мың(1000)

Mıñ(1000)

Ten Thousand(10,000)

Он мың(10,000)

On mıñ(10,000)

Hundred Thousand(100,000)

Жүз мың(100,000)

Jüz mıñ(100,000)

Million(1,000,000)

Миллион(1,000,000)

Mïllïon(1,000,000)

Billion(1,000,000,000)

Миллиард(1,000,000,000)

Mïllïard(1,000,000,000)

Ordinal Numbers
Реттік сандар
Rettik sandar

first
бірінші
birinşi

second
екінші
ekinşi

third
үшінші
üşinşi

fourth
төртінші
törtinşi

fifth
бесінші
besinşi

sixth
алтыншы
altınşı

seventh
жетінші
jetinşi

eighth

сегізінші

segizinşi

---

ninth

тоғызыншы

toğızınşı

---

tenth

оныншы

onınşı

---

eleventh

он бірінші

on birinşi

---

twelfth

он екінші

on ekinşi

---

thirteenth

он үшінші

on üşinşi

---

twentieth

жиырмасыншы

jiırmasınşı

---

twenty-first

жиырма бірінші

jiırma birinşi

hundredth

жүзінші

jüzinşi

thousandth

мыңыншы

mıñınşı

millionth

миллионыншы

mïllïonınşı

billionth

миллиардыншы

mïllïardınşı

Geometric Shapes
Геометриялық фигуралар
Geometrïyalıq fïguralar

angle

бұрыш

burış

circle

шеңбер

şeñber

cone

конус

konus

cube
куб
kub

cylinder
цилиндр
cilïndr

heart
жүрек
jürek

heptagon
жетібұрыш
jetiburış

hexagon
алтыбұрыш
altıburış

line
сызық
sızıq

octagon
сегізбұрыш
segizburış

oval
сопақ
sopaq

parallel lines

параллель сызықтар

parallel' sızıqtar

---

pentagon

бесбұрыш

besburış

---

perpendicular lines

перпендикуляр сызықтар

perpendïkulyar sızıqtar

---

polygon

көпбұрыш

köpburış

---

pyramid

пирамида

pïramïda

---

rectangle

тікбұрыш

tikburış

---

rhombus

ромб

romb

---

square

шаршы

şarşı

---

star

жұлдыз

juldız

---

trapezoid

трапеция

trapecïya

---

triangle

үшбұрыш

üşburış

---

vortex

құйын

quyın

Colors

Түстер

Tüster

---

beige

ақшыл сары

aqşıl sarı

---

black

қара

qara

---

blue

көк

kök

---

brown

қоңыр

qoñır

---

fuchsia

фуксия

fuksïya

---

gray

сұр

sur

---

green

жасыл

jasıl

---

indigo

күлгін көк

külgin kök

---

maroon

алқызыл

alqızıl

---

navy blue

қара көк

qara kök

---

orange

қызғылт сары

qızğılt sarı

---

pink

қызғылт

qızğılt

purple

күлгін

külgin

red

қызыл

qızıl

silver

күміс түсті

kümis tüsti

tan

сарғыш қоңыр

sarğış qoñır

teal

жасыл көк

jasıl kök

turquoise

көгілдір

kögildir

violet

күлгін

külgin

white

ақ

aq

---

yellow

сары

sarı

Related Verbs
Қатысты етістіктер
Qatıstı etistikter

to add

қосу

qosu

---

to change

өзгерту

özgertu

---

to check

тексеру

tekseru

---

to color

бояу

boyau

---

to count

есептеу

esepteu

---

to divide

бөлу

bölu

to figure

суреттеу

suretteu

to fill

толтыру

toltıru

to guess

болжамдау

boljamdau

to measure

өлшеу

ölşeu

to multiply

көбейту

köbeytu

to subtract

азайту

azaytu

to take

алу

alu

to tell time

уақытты айту

waqıttı aytu

---

to verify

растау

rastau

---

to watch

бақылау

baqılau

Michael is a **ten** year old boy who lives in Georgia. His family owns a **twenty acre** farm; he has **two** brothers and **three** sisters. Michael loves to work on his family's farm. He and his brothers wake up at **6:00 in the morning** every day. His favorite thing to do is ride his **brown** and **white** horse around the **perimeter** of the farm to check the fencing for damage. Even if there is only a **centimeter** of damaged wood, Michael must repair it. He also has to **measure** the **height** and **width** of the fence. He takes this job very seriously, so he doesn't want to miss a thing. Michael especially loves working on the farm in **autumn** because they sell more than **one thousand orange** pumpkins during the **month** of **October!** People from all over the state travel for **miles** to buy their pumpkins. Some of their pumpkins **weigh** as much as **one hundred pounds!** In the **winter**, his family sells Christmas trees. He loves helping other families find the perfect tree, whether it is **four feet**, **seven feet**, or even **nine feet tall!** In **December**, his family sells a **dozen green** trees a **day**, this keeps Michael very busy. In the **spring**, his family prepares the crops for the **summer** and autumn harvest. Because **spring** is such a busy **time** in school, each of the siblings take turns with special projects on the farm during the **week**; Michael's is the **first** day of the week, **Monday**; Henry's is the **second** day, **Tuesday**; Alan's is the **third** day, **Wednesday**; Sally's is the **fourth** day, **Thursday**; and Ann's is the **fifth** day, **Friday**. Little Ella is still too young for chores, but she loves to **measure** the **height** of the blooming **red** and **yellow** flowers with her **small ruler**. She is a **miniature** version of their mom. She cannot wait to grow up and help around the farm. During **summer**, Michael spends most of his **time** helping his mom cook. It is so hot outside, especially in **July** and **August**; he decided he needed a fun indoor activity. While cooking, he is learning how to convert different types of **measures**, like how many **teaspoons** are in a **tablespoon** and how many **cups** are in a **gallon**; he is also learning to add a **dash** here and **sprinkle** a **little** there to make the recipe just right. Mom knows cooking is a good skill to learn, but she also knows he will be learning these **measurements** in school this **September**.

Майкл Джорджияда тұратын **он** жасар бала.Оның жанұясы **жиырма акр** фермаға ие; оның **екі** ағасы және **үш** апасы бар.

Майкл өз жанұясының фермасында жұмыс жасағанды ұнатады.

Ол және оның ағалары күнде **таңғы 6:00** тұрады. Оның сүйікті ісі – **қоңыр ала** атпен қоршаудың бұзылғандығын тексеру үшін ферма **периметрі** айналасында жүру. Егер ағаштың тіпті 1 **сантиметрі** ғана бұзылса да, Майкл оны жөндеуге міндетті. Сонымен қатар, ол дуалдың **ұзындығы** мен **енін өлшеуі** тиіс. Майкл бұл іске өте жауапты қарайды, сондықтан ол ештеңені өткізіп алғысы келмейді. Майкл фермада **күзде** жұмыс жасағанды ерекше ұнатады, өйткені олар **бір мыңнан астам қызылт сары** асқабақтарды **Қазан айында** сатып шығады! Штаттың барлық жерінен адамдар олардың асқабақтарын сатып алу үшін бірнеше **миля** саяхаттап келеді. Олардың кейбір асқабақтарының **салмағы бір жүз фунтқа** дейін жетеді! **Қыста** оның жанұясы Рождество шыршаларын сатады. Ол басқа жанұяларға мінсіз шырша табуға көмектескенді ұнатады, оларадың **ұзындығы төрт фут, жеті фут,** кейде тіпті **тоғыз фут** болса да! **Желтоқсанда** оның жанұясы **бір күнде он екі жасыл талдан** сатады, бұл істен Майклдың қолы босамайды. **Көктемде** оның жанұясы **жазғы** және **күзгі** өнімге егістерді дайындайды. Көктемде мектептен бос **уақыты** болмағандықтан, туған ағайындылар апта бойына фермада арнайы жоспар бойынша алмасып тұрады. Майклдікі **аптаның бірінші** күні, **Дүйсенбі;** Генридікі **екінші** күн, **Сейсінбі;** Аландікі **үшінші** күн, **Сәрсенбі;** Саллидікі **төртінші** күн, **Бейсенбі;** және Аннанікі **бесінші** күн, **Жұма.** Кішкене Эла үй жұмысына әлі де кішкентай, бірақ ол өзінің **кішкентай сызғышымен** гүлдеп тұрған **қызыл** және **сары** гүлдердің **ұзындығын өлшегенді** ұнатады. Ол олардың анасының **кішігірім** түрі. Ферма жұмысына көмектесу үшін ол өскенше күте тұра алмайды. Жаз бойына Майкл өзінің көп **уақытын** анасына ас әзірлеуге көмектесуге жұмсайды. Ауа райы қатты ыстық, әсіресе **шілде** мен **тамызда;** Сондықтан ол үй іші белсенділігін қызықтауды ұйғарды. Ас әзірлеу барысында ол **ас қасықтың** ішінде қанша **шай қасық** болатыны және **галлонда** қанша **кесе** болатыны сияқты **өлшемдердің** әр түрін айналдыруды үйреніп жүр.

Сонымен қатар, ол рецепт дұрыс болу үшін бір жеріне **мысқал** қосып және басқа жеріне **аз ғана себуді** үйреніп жатыр. Анасы ас әзірлеу дағдылануға жақсы кәсіп екенін біледі, бірақ сонымен қатар, ол осы **өлшемдерді** мектепте осы **қыркүйекте** үйренетіндігін біледі.

Maykl Jordjïyada turatın **on** jasar bala. Onıñ januyası **jïırma akr** fermağa ïe. Onıñ eki ağası jäne **üş** apası bar. Maykl öz januyasınıñ fermasında jumıs jasağandı unatadı. Ol jäne onıñ ağaları künde **tañği 6:00** turadı. Onıñ süyikti isi – **qoñır ala** atpen qorşaudıñ buzılğandığın tekseru üşin ferma **perïmetri** aynalasında şabu. Eger ağaştıñ tipti 1 **santïmetri** ğana buzılsa da, Maykl onı jöndeuge mindetti. Sonımen qatar, ol dualdıñ **uzındığı** men **enin ölşeui** tïis. Maykl bul iske öte jauaptı qaraydı, sondıqtan ol eşteñeni ötkizip alğısı kelmeydi. Maykl fermada **küzde** jumıs jasağandı erekşe unatadı, öytkeni olar **bir mıñnan astam qızılt sarı** asqabaqtardı **Qazan ayında** satıp şığadı! Şattıñ barlıq jerinen adamdar olardıñ asqabaqtarın satyp alu üşin birneşe **mïlya** sayaxattap keledi. Olardıñ keybir asqabaqtarınıñ **salmağı bir jüz funtqa** deyin jetedi! **Qısta** onıñ januyası Rojdestvo şırşaların satadı. Ol basqa januyalarğa minsiz şırşa tabuğa kömekteskendi unatadı, olaradıñ **uzındığı tört fut**, **jeti fut**, keyde tipti **toğız fut** bolsa da! **Jeltoqsanda** onıñ januyası bir **künde on eki jasyl taldan** satadı, bul isten Maykldıñ qolı bosamaydı. **Köktemde** onıñ januyası **jazğı** jäne **küzgi** önimge egisterdi dayındaydı. Köktemde mektepten bos **waqyty** bolmagandıqtan, tuğan ağayındılar apta boyına fermada arnayı jospar boyınşa almasıp turadı. Maykldiki **aptanıñ birinşi** küni, **Düysenbi**; Genrïdiki **ekinşi** kün, **Seysinbi**; Alandiki **üşinşi** kün, **Särsenbi**; Sallïdiki **törtinşi** kün, **Beysenbi**; jäne Annaniki **besinşi** kün, **Juma**. Kişkene Élla üy jumısına äli de kişkentay, biraq ol öziniñ

kişkentay sızğışımen güldep turğan **qızıl** jäne **sarı** gülderdiñ **uzındığın ölşegendi** unatadı. Ol olardıñ anasınıñ **kişigirim** türi. Ferma jumısına kömektesu üşin ol öskenşe küte tura almaydı. Jaz boyına Maykl öziniñ köp **waqıtın** anasına as äzirleuge kömektesuge jumsaydı Awa rayı qattı ıstıq, äsirese **şilde** men **tamızda**; Sondıqtan ol üy işi belsendiligin qızıqtaudı uyğardı. As äzirleu barısında ol **as qasıqtıñ** işinde qanşa **şay qasıq** bolatıny jäne **gallonda** qanşa **kese** bolatıny sıyaqtı **ölşemderdiñ** är türin aynaldırudı üyrenip jur.

Sonımen qatar, ol recept durıs bolu üşin bir jerine **mısqal** qosıp jäne basqa jerine **az ğana sebudi** üyrenip jatır. Anası as äzirleu dağdılanuğa jaqsı käsip ekenin biledi, biraq sonımen qatar, ol osı **ölşemderdi** mektepte osı **qırküyekte** üyrenetindigin biledi.

2) Weather
2) Ауа райы
2) Awa rayı

air
ауа
awa

---

atmosphere
атмосфера
atmosfera

---

avalanche
көшкін
köşkin

---

barometer
барометр
barometr

---

barometric pressure
атмосфералық қысым
atmosferalıq qısım

---

blizzard
боран
boran

---

breeze

самал жел

samal jel

climate

климат

klïmat

cloud

бұлт

bult

cold

суық

suıq

cold front

суық фронт

suıq front

condensation

конденсация

kondensacïya

cool

салқын

salqın

cyclone

циклон

cïklon

degree

градус

gradus

---

depression

жабығу

jabığu

---

dew

шық

şıq

---

dew point

шық нүктесі

şıq nüktesi

---

downpour

нөсер

nöser

---

drift

ауытқу

awıtqu

---

drizzle

ақ жаңбыр

aq jañbır

---

drought

құрғақшылық

qurğaqşılıq

dry

құрғақ

qurğaq

dust devil

тозаңды құйын

tozañdı quyın

duststorm

тозаңды дауыл

tozañdı dauıl

easterly wind

шығыс желі

şığıs jeli

evaporation

булану

bulanu

eye of the storm

дауыл көзі

dauıl közi

fair

жәрмеңке

järmeñke

fall

құлау

qulau

flash flood

кенет тасқын

kenet tasqın

flood

тасқын

tasqın

flood stage

тасқын деңгейі

tasqın deñgeyi

flurries

нөсерлер

nöserler

fog

тұман

tuman

forecast

болжам

boljam

freeze

қатыру

qatıru

freezing rain

мұздай жаңбыр

muzday jañbır

front (cold/hot)

(салқын/ыстық) фронт

(calqın/ıstıq) front

---

frost

аяз

ayaz

---

funnel cloud

құбыр тәріздес

qubır tärizdes

---

global warming

глобалдық жылыну

globaldıq jılınu

---

gust of wind

жел екпіні

jel ekpini

---

hail

бұршақ

burşaq

---

haze

тұман

tuman

---

heat

жылу

jılu

---

heat index

жылу индексі

jılu ïndeksi

heat wave

жылу толқыны

jılu tolqını

high

жоғары

joğarı

humid

ылғал

ilğal

humidity

ылғалдылық

ılğaldılıq

hurricane

қатты дауыл

qattı dauıl

ice

мұз

muz

ice crystals

мұз кристалдары

muz krïstaldarı

ice storm
боран
boran

icicle
сүңгі
süñgi

jet stream
реактивті ағын
reaktïvti ağın

landfall
жағаға жетеберіс
jağağa jeteberis

lightning
найзағай
nayzağay

low
төмен
tömen

low pressure system
төменгі қысым жүйесі
tömengi qısım jüyesi

meteorologist
метеоролог
meteorolog

meteorology

метеорология

meteorologïya

---

microburst

шағын жарылыс

şağın jarılıs

---

mist

тұман

tuman

---

moisture

ылғал

ılğal

---

monsoon

муссон

musson

---

muggy

тымырсық

tımırsıq

---

nor'easter

солтүстік-шығыс

soltüstik-şığıs

---

normal

қалыпты

qalıptı

---

outlook

көрініс

körinis

overcast

бұлыңғыр

bulıñğır

ozone

озон

ozon

partly cloudy

ішінара бұлтты

işinara bulttı

polar

полярлық

polyarlıq

pollutant

ластауыш

lastauış

precipitation

жауын-шашын

jauın-şaşın

pressure

қысым

qısım

radar

радар

radar

---

radiation

радиация

radïacïya

---

rain

жаңбыр

jañbır

---

rainbow

кемпірқосақ

kempirqosaq

---

rain gauge

жаңбыр мөлшері

jañbır mölşeri

---

relative humidity

біркелкі ылғалдылық

birkelki ılğaldılıq

---

sandstorm

құм дауыл

qum dauıl

---

season

мезгіл

mezgil

shower

нөсерлі

nöserli

---

sky

аспан

aspan

---

sleet

қарлы жаңбыр

qarlı jañbır

---

slush

лайсаң

laysañ

---

smog

тозаң қоспасы

tozañ qospası

---

smoke

түтін

tütin

---

snow

қар

qar

---

snowfall

қар жауу

qar jauu

---

snowflake

қар ұшқыны

qar uşqını

---

snow flurry

қар түсу

qar tüsu

---

snow shower

қар басу

qar basu

---

snowstorm

боран

boran

---

spring

көктем

köktem

---

storm

дауыл

dauıl

---

storm surge

дауыл толқыны

dauıl tolqını

---

stratosphere

стратосфера

stratosfera

---

summer

жаз

jaz

---

sunrise

күн шығуы

kün şığuı

---

sunset

күн батуы

kün batuı

---

supercell

найзағай

nayzağay

---

surge

толқын

tolqın

---

swell

толқындар

tolqındar

---

temperature

температура

temperatura

---

thaw

жылымық

jılımıq

---

thermal

жылыл**ы**қ

jılılıq

thermometer

терм**о**метр

termometr

thunder

к**ү**н күркір**е**у

kün kürkireu

thunderstorm

найза**ғ**ай

nayzağay

tornado

кұй**ы**н

kuyın

trace

і**з**

iz

tropical

тр**о**пиктік

tropïktik

tropical depression

тр**о**пиктік жабы**ғ**у

tropïktik jabığu

tropical storm

тропиктік дауыл

tropïktik dauıl

---

turbulence

турбуленттік

turbulenttik

---

twister

құйын

quyın

---

typhoon

тайфун

tayfun

---

unstable

тұрақсыз

turaqsız

---

visibility

көз көрерлік

köz körerlik

---

vortex

қатты жел

qattı jel

---

warm

жылы

jılı

---

warning

ескерту

eskertu

watch

бақылау

baqılau

weather

ауа райы

awa rayı

wether pattern

ауа райы картасы

awa rayı kartası

weather report

ауа райы туралы мағлұмат

awa rayı turalı mağlumat

weather satellite

ауа райы серігі

awa rayı serigi

westerly wind

батыс желі

batıs jeli

whirlwind

қатты жел

qattı jel

wind

жел

jel

---

wind chill

жел суықтығы

jel suıqtığı

---

winter

қыс

qıs

Related Verbs
Қатысты етістіктер

Qatıstı etistikter

to blow

соғу

soğu

---

to clear up

тазарту

tazartu

---

to cool down

мұздау

muzdau

---

to drizzle

сіркіреу

sirkireu

---

to feel

сезілу

sezilu

---

to forecast

болжау

boljau

---

to hail

бұршақ жауу

burşaq jauu

---

to rain

жаңбыр жауу

jañbır jauu

---

to report

хабарлау

xabarlau

---

to shine

жарқырау

jarqırau

---

to snow

қар жауу

qar jauu

---

to storm

дауыл соғу

dauıl soğu

---

to warm up

жылыну

jılınu

---

to watch

бақылау

baqılau

Heather loves the **seasons** and **weather**. She dreams of one day becoming a **meteorologist** so she can share her love with everyone. She is currently attending school to study the **weather** and how it works. She is learning that each of the four **seasons** brings its own **weather patterns** to the world. She is amazed at how the **seasons** affect the **weather**. The **seasons** vary throughout the world, but here in America, where Heather lives, there are four distinct **seasons**, and each of them brings something different to our world. In **winter**, the **temperature** is **cold** and the ground is white with **snow**. The **wind** gets so **cold** up on the mountaintop that the **wind chill** is below zero **degrees**. Sometimes, the **wind** blows with such force that it causes an **avalanche** of **snow** on the mountain. When the **air** is this **cold**, you are likely to wake up with **frost** on your car. In the **spring**, things begin to **heat** up. The **temperature** begins to **warm** up a bit, making the **snow** on the ground **thaw** out. The flowers begin to bloom and the trees begin to grow leaves. **Spring** often brings **rain**; sometimes the **rain** is so heavy, it causes **flash floods**. A common sighting in spring is a beautiful **rainbow** after the **rain**. The **temperature** is **hot** in the **summer**. The **temperatures** begin to rise and the **heat index** goes up causing a **heat wave**. There is not much **precipitation** in **summer**; however, occasionally the **clouds** bring a **thunderstorm**. The **rain** usually does not last long in **summer**, but the **thunder** and **lightning** can be dangerous. Every time there is a **thunderstorm**, Heather will watch the **weather report** to see if they will issue a **watch** or a **warning**. After **summer**, **fall** brings the start of **cool temperatures**. The leaves on the trees begin to fall, preparing the tree for the **winter**. In the coastal regions, **hurricanes** become a problem in the **fall**. This is a dangerous, yet exciting time in the world of **meteorology**. The **seasons** have a huge effect on **weather**; however the biggest changes in **weather** and the most dangerous events, such as **tsunamis**, **tornados**, and **storms**, occur during the change in **seasons**. The **unstable** and ever-changing **temperatures** affect the **barometric pressure** in a way that causes these types of events. While dangerous, they are exciting to someone like Heather who studies the **weather**. Heather's goal is to one day help educate and warn people in advance when these events are likely to occur.

Хизер **мезгілдер** мен **ауа райын** ұнатады. Ол бір күні **метеоролог** болып, өзінің махаббатымен барлық адамдармен бөлісуді армандайды. Ол қазір **ауа райын** зерттеу және оның қалай жұмыс жасайтынын білу үшін мектепте оқып жүр. Ол әр **мезгіл** әлемге өзінің **ауа райы картасын** алып келетіндігін зерттеп жатыр. Ол **мезгілдердің ауа райына** қалай әсер ететіне таң қалады. Әлемде **мезгілдер** әрқилы, бірақ осы Америкада, Хизердің тұратын жерінде төрт түрлі **мезгілдер** болады және олардың әрқайсысы біздің әлемге ерекше өзгерістер әкеледі. **Қыста температура суық** және жер беті **қармен** ақ. Тау шыңдарында **жел суық** болатындығы сонша **жел суықтығы** нөл **градустан** төмен болады. Кейде **желдің** қатты соғатындығы сонша, таулардағы **қар көшкініне** алып келеді. **Ауа суық** болған жағдайда, таңертеңгісін машинаны **аяз** басқанын байқар едіңіз. **Көктемде** барлығы **жылына** бастайды. **Температура** аздап **жыли** бастап, жер бетіндегі **қарды еріте** бастайды. Гүлдер гүлдене бастайды және талдарда жапырақтар өсе бастайды. **Көктем** жиі **жаңбыр** әкеледі. Кейде **жаңбырдың** ауырлығы сонша, **кенеттен тасқынға** айналады. **Көктемдегі** жалпы бақылау – **жаңбырдан** кейінгі әдемі **кемпірқосақ**. **Жазда температура** ыстық. **Температура** өсе бастайды және **жылу индексі** көтеріліп **қатты ыстық кезеңін** тудырады. **Жазда жауын-шашын** көп болмайды, бірақ кейде **бұлттар найзағай** алып келеді. Әдетте, **жазда жаңбыр** ұзақ жаумайды.бірақ **күн күркіреу** мен **найзағай** қауіпті болуы мүмкін. Бұл жерде әрдайым күн күркірейді. Хизер **ауа райы туралы мағлұматты** олардың **бақылаулар** мен **ескертулер** шығарғанын көру үшін қарайтын болады. **Жаздан** кейін, **күз суық температураның** басын бастайды. Талдағы жапырақтар түсе бастайды, бұл талдарды **қысқа** дайындайды. Жағалауға жақын аудандарда **күзде дауыл** проблема болып табылады. Бұл өте қауіпті, алайда **метеорология** әлемі үшін өте тартымды уақыт. **Мезгілдер ауа райына** елеулі әсер етеді. Алайда, **ауа райындағы** үлкен өзгерістер және **цунами, торнадо, дауыл** сияқты өте қауіпті **құбылыстар мезгілдердің** ішіндегі өзгерістер барысында пайда болады. **Тұрақсыз** және жиі өзгеріп тұратын **температуралар** өз жолында **атмосфералық қысымға** әсер етеді және ол осындай сияқты құбылыстарға әкеледі. Қауіпті бола тұра, олар **ауа райын** зерттейтін Хизер сияқты қызға қызықты болады.Хизердің мақсаты бір күні осындай құбылыстар болған жағдайда адамдарды үйретіп және алдын ала ескерту.

Xïzer **mezgilder** men **awa rayın** unatadı. Ol bir küni **meteorolog** bolıp, öziniñ maxabbatımen barlıq adamdarmen bölisudi armandaydı. Ol qazir **awa rayın** zerttew jäne onıñ qalay jumıs jasaytının bilu üşin mektepte oqıp jür. Ol är **mezgil** älemge öziniñ **awa rayı kartasın** alıp keletindigin zerttep jatır. Ol **mezgilderdiñ awa rayına** qalay äser etetine tañ qaladı. Älemde **mezgilder** ärqïlı, biraq osı Amerïkada, Xïzerdiñ turatın jerinde tört türli **mezgilder** boladı jäne olardıñ ärqaysısı bizdiñ älemge erekşe özgerister äkeledi. **Qısta temperatura suıq** jäne jer beti **qarmen** aq. Tau şıñdarında **jel suıq** bolatındığı sonşa **jel suıqtığı** nol' **gradustan** tömen boladı. Keyde **jeldiñ** qattı soğatındığı sonşa, taulardağı **qar köşkinine** alıp keledi. **Awa suıq** bolğan jağdayda, tañerteñgisin maşinanı **ayaz** basqanın bayqar ediñiz. **Köktemde** barlığı **jılına** bastaydı. **Temperatura** azdap **jılï** bastap, jer betindegi **qardı erite** bastaydı. Gülder güldene bastaydı jäne taldarda japıraqtar öse bastaydı. **Köktem** jïi **jañbır** äkeledi. Keyde **jañbırdıñ** auırlığı sonşa, **kenetten tasqınğa** aynaladı. **Köktemdegi** jalpı baqılau – **jañbırdan** keyingi ädemi **kempirqosaq. Jazda temperatura** ıstıq. **Temperatura** öse bastaydı jäne **jılu ïndeksi** köterilip **qattı ıstıq kezeñin** tudıradı. Jazda **jawın-şaşın** köp bolmaydı, biraq keyde **bulttar nayzağay** alıp keledi. Ädette, **jazda jañbır** uzaq jaumaydı.biraq **kün kürkireu** men **nayzağay** qauipti boluı mümkin. Bul jerde ärdayım **kün kürkireydi.** Xïzer **awa rayı** turalı mağlumattı olardıñ **baqılaular** men **eskertuler** şığarğanın köru üşin qaraytın boladı. **Jazdan** keyin, **küz suıq temperaturanıñ** basın bastaydı. Taldağı japıraqtar tüse bastaydı, bul taldardı **qısqa** dayındaydı. Jağalauğa jaqın audandarda **küzde dauıl** problema bolıp tabıladı. Bul öte qauipti, alayda **meteorologïya** älemi üşin öte tartımdı waqıt. **Mezgilder awa rayına** eleuli äser etedi. Alayda, **awa rayındağı** ülken özgerister jäne

cunamï, **tornado**, **dauıl** sïyaqtı öte qauipti qubılıstar **mezgilderdiñ** işindegi özgerister barısında payda boladı. **Turaqsız** jäne jii özgerip turatın **temperaturalar** öz jolında **atmosferalıq qısımğa** äser etedi jäne ol osınday sïyaqtı qubılıstarğa äkeledi. Qauipti bola tura, olar **awa rayın** zertteytin Xizer sïyaqtı qızğa qızıqtı boladı.Xizerdiñ maqsatı bir küni osınday qubılıstar bolğan jağdayda adamdardı üyretip jäne aldın ala eskertu.

3) People
3) Адамдар
3) Adamdar

athlete

атлет

atlet

baby

нәресте

näreste

boy

ұл

ul

boyfriend

дос жігіт

dos jigit

brother

аға

ağa

brother-in-law

жезде

jezde

businessman

кәсіпкер

käsipker

candidate

үміткер

ümitker

child/children

бала/балалар

bala/balalar

coach

бапкер

bapker

cousin

бөле, жиен

böle, jïen

customer

клиент

klïent

daughter

қыз

qız

daughter-in-law

келін

kelin

driver

жүргізуші

jürgizuşi

---

family

жанұя

januya

---

farmer

фермер

fermer

---

father/dad

әке

äke

---

father-in-law

ата

ata

---

female

әйел

äyel

---

friend

дос

dos

---

girl

қыз

qız

---

girlfriend

дос қыз

dos qız

godparents

кіндік ата-ана

kindik ata-ana

grandchildren

немерелер

nemereler

granddaughter

немере

nemere

grandfather

ата

ata

grandmother

әже

äje

grandparents

ата-әже

ata-äje

grandson

немере

nemere

husband

күйеу

küyeu

---

instructor

нұсқаушы

nusqauşı

---

kid

бөбек

böbek

---

king

патша

patşa

---

male

еркек

erkek

---

man

адам/ер

adam/er

---

mother/mom

ана

ana

---

mother-in-law

ене

ene

---

nephew

немере іні/жиен

nemere ini/jïen

niece

немере қарындас/жиен

nemere qarındas/jïen

parent

ата-ана

ata-ana

people

адамдар

adamdar

princess

ханшайым

xanşayım

queen

ханым

xanım

rock star

рок жұлдызы

rok juldızı

sister

апа

apa

sister-in-law

қай**ын** сіңлі

qayın siñli

son

ұл

ul

son-in-law

күй**е**у бал**а**

küyew bala

student

студ**е**нт

student

teenager

ж**а**с өспірім

jas öspirim

tourist

тур**ис**т/саяхатш**ы**

turïst/ sayaxatşı

wife

әй**е**л

äyel

woman

әй**е**л

äyel

youth

жастар

jastar

Characteristic
Сипаттама
Sïpattama

---

attractive

тартымды

tartımdı

---

bald

таз

taz

---

beard

сақал

saqal

---

beautiful

әдемі

ädemi

---

black hair

қара шаш

qara şaş

---

blind

соқыр

soqır

---

blond

сары шашты

sarı şaştı

---

blue eyes

көк көздер

kök közder

---

brown eyes

қоңыр көздер

qoñır közder

---

brown hair

қоңыр шаш

qoñır şaş

---

brunette

қара шашты

qara şaştı

---

curly hair

бұйра шашты

buyra şaştı

---

dark

қара қоңыр

qara qoñır

---

deaf

саңырау

sañırau

---

divorced

ажырасқан

ajırasqan

elderly

қарт

qart

fair (skin)

ақсары

aqsarı

fat

толық

tolıq

gray hair

сұр шашты

sur şaştı

green eyes

жасыл көздер

jasıl közder

handsome

сұлу

sulu

hazel eyes

қоңыр көздер

qoñır közder

heavyset

ірі

iri

---

light brown

ақшыл қоңыр

aqşıl qoñır

---

long hair

ұзын шаш

uzın şaş

---

married

үйленген

üylengen

---

mustache

мұрт

murt

---

old

жасы үлкен

jası ülken

---

olive

сұрғыш жасыл

surğış jasıl

---

overweight

артық салмақты

artıq salmaqty

---

pale

боз

boz

petite

кішігірім

kişigirim

plump

томпақ

tompaq

pregnant

жүкті

jükti

red head

жирен

jïren

short

қысқа

qısqa

short hair

қысқа шаш

qısqa şaş

skinny

арық

arıq

slim
сымбатты
sımbattı

stocky
мығым
mığım

straight hair
тік шаш
tik şaş

tall
ұзын
uzın

tanned
күнге күйген
künge küygen

thin
жұқа
juqa

wavy hair
бұйра шаш
buyra şaş

well built
жақсы бітімді
jaqsı bitimdi

white

ақ

aq

---

young

жас

jas

Stages of Life
Өмір кезеңдері
Ömir kezeñderi

adolescence

жастық

jastıq

---

adult

ересек

eresek

---

anniversary

жылдық

jıldıq

---

birth

дүниеге келу

dünïege kelu

---

death

өлім

ölim

---

divorce

ажырасу

ajırasu

---

elderly

жасы үлкен

jası ülken

---

graduation

оқу бітіру

oqu bitiru

---

infant

сәби

säbï

---

marriage

үйлену

üylenu

---

middle aged

орта жас

orta jas

---

newborn

нәресте

näreste

---

preschooler

мектеп жасына дейінгі бала

mektep jasına deyingi bala

---

preteen

жас өспірім жасына дейінгі бала

jas öspirim jasına deyingi bala

---

senior citizen

зейнеткер

zeynetker

---

teenager

жас өспірім

jas öspirim

---

toddler

балдырған

baldırğan

---

tween

егіз

egiz

---

young adult

ержеткен/бойжеткен

erjetken/boyjetken

---

youth

жастар

jastar

Religion
Дін

Din

Atheist

Атеист

Ateïst

Agnostic

Агностик

Agnostïk

Baha'i

Бахаизм

Baxaïzm

Buddhist

Буддист

Buddïst

Christian

Христиан

Xrïstïan

Hindu

Индуист

Induïst

Jewish

Жебірей

Jebirey

Muslim

Мұсылман

Musılman

Sikh

Сикх

Sïkx

Work

Жұмыс

Jumıs

accountant

есепші

esepşi

---

actor

актёр

aktyor

---

associate

серіктес

seriktes

---

astronaut

ғарышкер

ğarışker

---

banker

банкир

bankïr

---

butcher

қасапшы

qasapşı

---

carpenter

ағаш ұстасы

ağaş ustası

---

chef

аспазшы

aspazşı

---

clerk

клерк

klerk

---

composer

сазгер

sazger

---

custodian

қамқоршы

saqtauşı

---

dentist

тіс дәрігері

tis därigeri

---

doctor

дәрігер

däriger

---

electrician
электрші
élektrşi

---

executive
басшы
basşı

---

farmer
фермер
fermer

---

fireman
өрт сөндіруші
ört söndiruşi

---

handyman
шебер
şeber

---

judge
төреші
töreşi

---

landscaper
бағбан
bağban

---

lawyer
адвокат
advokat

---

librarian

кітапханашы

kitapxanaşı

manager

менеджер

menejer

model

модель

model'

notary

нотариус

notarïus

nurse

медбике

medbïke

optician

оптик

optïk

pharmacist

фармацевт

farmacevt

pilot

ұшқыш

uşqış

policeman

полиция қызметкері

polïcïya qïzmetkeri

---

preacher

уағызшы

waǧïzşı

---

president

президент

prezïdent

---

representative

өкіл

ökil

---

scientist

ғалым

ĝalım

---

secretary

хатшы

xatşı

---

singer

әнші

änşi

---

soldier

әскер

äsker

---

teacher

мұғалім

muğalim

---

technician

техникалық маман

texnïkalıq maman

---

treasurer

қазынашы

qazınaşı

---

writer

жазушы

jazuşı

---

zoologist

зоолог

zoolog

Related Verbs
Қатысты етістіктер

Qatıstı etistikter

---

to deliver

жеткізу

jetkizu

---

to enjoy

рахаттану

raxattanu

---

to grow

өсу

ösu

to laugh

күлу

külu

to love

сүю/жақсы көру

süyu/jaqsı köru

to make

жасау

jasau

to manage

басқару

basqaru

to repair

жөндеу

jöndeu

to serve

қызмет ету

qızmet etu

to sing

ән айту

än aytu

to smile
күлімдеу
külimdeu

to talk
сөйлесу
söylesu

to think
ойлау
oylau

to work
жұмыс жасау
jumıs jasau

to work at
бір жерде жұмыс жасау
bir jerde jumıs jasau

to work for
белгілі уақыт аралығында жұмыс жасау
belgili waqıt aralığında jumıs jasau

to work on
бір затқа ұмтылу
bir zatqa umtılu

to worship
сыйлау
sıylau

to write

жазу

jazu

John is a successful **pilot** and **businessman**. This came as no surprise to any of his **family** and **friends**, but his start in life wasn't an easy one. When he was just a **baby**, John spent a lot of time seeing **doctors** for a rare condition he was born with. As an **infant**, he was very sick and required the care of a **nurse** all the time. While he was in the hospital, everyone came to visit him; **aunts**, **uncles**, **cousins**, and of course his **grandparents**. Finally, he got well and he was able to live a normal, healthy life. Because of all he had been through, his **parents** knew he would be a successful **man**. As a **toddler**, he and his **grandfather** loved to watch planes fly over his house. John's **grandfather** told his **grandson** that he could be anything he wanted when he grew up. He was such a curious **child**, but never lost his love of planes, he even dreamed of being an **astronaut**. As he grew older, he really excelled in math and science class, his **teachers** were amazed and his **mom** and **dad** were so proud of him. He was the top **student** in his class when he graduated high school. He was a **tall**, **handsome young man** with **black hair** and **blue eyes**. He was also very talented on the basketball court; his **coach** thought he was a fine **youth** as well. He was just a **teenager** when he finished college and became a **pilot**, finally getting to live his lifelong dream. One day there was an accident that forced John into the hospital for quite some time, there he met a young **woman** named Rachel, and she was a **nurse.** John quickly recovered under the care of his **girlfriend**, but he was never able to fly again. He did however become a flight school

instructor where he was able to teach other people how to fly. It wasn't long that John and Rachel because **husband** and **wife.** They had two lovely **children,** one **boy** and one **girl.** Jill is quite the **singer**; everything is a microphone to this aspiring **rock star.** She is the cutest little **princess** you have ever seen! But Little Johnny Junior is following in his **father's** footsteps because he dreams of being a **pilot,** just like his **daddy. Father, son,** and **grandson** all love to spend quiet Sunday afternoons watching the planes go by. John knows that one day his **son** will be able to fly planes just like he did. While this thought scares him a little because of the accident, he is very proud of his **son** for his passion for flying. Maybe one day he will be a **student** in his **father's** flight school. In all of his successes, John's **family** is the achievement he is most proud of.

Джон табысты **ұшқыш** және **кәсіпкер.** Оның осындай болғанына **жанұясы** мен **достары** таң қалған жоқ, алайда оның өмірі оңайлықпен басталған жоқ. Ол **кішкентай** кезінде туылған сирек жағдайы үшін **дәрігерлермен** кездесуге көп уақытын жұмсады. Ол **сәби** болған кезінде қатты ауырды және әрдайым **медбикенің** күтімін қажетсінді. Ол ауруханада жатқан кезде барлығы оның көңілін сұрауға келетін: **ағалары, апалары, бөлелері** және әрине **ата-әжелері.** Нәтижесінде, оның жағдайы жақсарып, ол қалыпты және сау өмір сүре алатын болды. Ол осындай қиындықтарды жеңіп шыққандықтан, оның **ата-анасы** оның жетістігі мол **адам** болатынын білді. **Балдырған** шағында ол **атасымен** үйдің үстінен ұшқан ұшақтарды бақылағанды ұнататын. Джонның **атасы** өзінің **немересіне** ол өскенде қалаған маман иесі бола алатынын айтты. Ол сондай қызыққұмар **бала** болатын, бірақ ешқашан ұшақтарға деген махаббатын жоғалтпады, тіптен **ғарышкер** болуды армандайтын. Ол есейгенде, математика мен ғылым сабақтарынан көріне бастады, **мұғалімдер** оған таң қалып, ал **ата-анасы** оны мақтаныш тұтатын. Ол орта мектепті бітірген кезде өз класының үздік **оқушысы** болды. Ол бойы **ұзын, қара шашты, көк көзді сұлу жас жігіт** болды. Сонымен қатар, ол баскетбол алаңында да өте талантты болатын. Оның **бапкері** оны сондай-ақ тамаша **жас жігіт** деп есептейтін. Нәтижесінде оның өмір бойы армандаған мақсаты орындалып, колледж бітіріп, **ұшқыш** болған кезінде ол әлі **жас өспірім** еді. Бір күні апат орын алып, ол ауруханада біраз уақыт жатуға мәжбүр болды. Бұл жерде ол Рейчел атты жас **әйелді** кездестіреді және ол **медбике** болып жұмыс жасады. Джон өзінің **дос қызының** күтімімен тез жазылып кетеді, алайда ол ешқашан ұша алмайтын болады. Алайда ол басқа адамдарды ұшуға үйрету үшін ұшу мектебінің **нұсқаушысы** болады. Арада көп ұзамай, Рэйчел мен Джон **ерлі-зайыпты** атанады. Олардың екі сүйкімді балалары болады, бір ұл және бір қыз. Джилл- нағыз әнші. Рок жұлдызы болуға ұмтылған қызға бәрі де микрофонға айналады. Ол бұрын соңды сіз көрмеген ең сүйкімді кішкентай ханшайым. Бірақ кішкентай кіші Джонни **әкесінің** ізін баспақшы, өйткені ол дәл **әкесі** сияқты **ұшқыш** болуды армандайды. **Әкесі, баласы** және **немересі** тынық жексенбі түсінде ұшып бара жатқан ұшақтарды бақылағанды ұнатады. Джон **баласының** бір күні өзі секілді ұшақтарды ұшыра алатынын біледі. Бірақ мұндай ойлар кезінде апат салдарынан қорқыныш туындайды, алайда ол баласының ұшқыш болу ұмтылысын мақтаныш тұтады. Мүмкін бір күні ол **әкесінің** ұшу мектебінің **студенті** болар. Оның барлық жетістіктерінің ішіндегі Джонның **жануясы**- ерекше мақтан тұтатын жетістігі.

Jon tabıstı **uşqış** jäne **käsipker**. Onıñ osınday bolğanına **januyası** men **dostarı** tañ qalğan joq, alayda onıñ ömiri oñaylıqpen bastalğan joq. Ol **bala** kezinde tuılğan sirek jağdayı üşin **därigerlermen** kezdesuge köp waqıtın jumsadı. Ol **säbï** bolğan kezinde qattı auırdı jäne ärdayım **medbïkeniñ** kütimin qajetsindi. Ol auruxanada jatqan kezde barlığı onıñ köñilin surauğa keletin: **ağaları**, **apaları**, **böleleri** jäne äriñe **ata-äjeleri**. Nätïjesinde, onıñ jağdayı jaqsarıp, ol qalıptı jäne sau ömir süre alatın boldı. Ol osınday qïndıqtardı jeñip şıqqandıqtan, onıñ **ata-anası** onıñ jetistigi mol **adam** bolatının bildi. **Baldırğan** şağında ol **atasımen** üydiñ üstinen uşqan uşaqtardı baqılağandı unatatın. Jonnıñ **atası** öziniñ **nemeresine** ol öskende qalağan maman ïesi bola alatının aytty. Ol sonday qızıqqumar **bala** bolatın, biraq eşqaşan uşaqtarğa degen maxabbatın joğaltpady, tipten **ğarışker** boludı armandaytın. Ol eseygende, matematïka men ğılım sabaqtarınan körine bastadı, **muğalimder** oğan tañ qalıp, al **ata-anası** onı maqtanış tutatın. Ol orta mektepti bitirgen kezde öz klasınıñ üzdik **oquşısı** boldı. Ol boyı **uzın**, **qara şaştı**, **kök közdi sulu jas jigit** boldı. Sonımen qatar, ol basketbol alañında da öte talanttı bolatın. Onıñ **bapkeri** onı sonday-aq tamaşa **jas jigit** dep esepteytin. Nätïjesinde onıñ ömir boyı armandağan maqsatı orındalıp, kolledj bitirip, **uşqış** bolğan kezinde ol äli **jas öspirim** edi. Bir küni apat orın alıp, ol auruxanada biraz waqıt jatuğa mäjbür boldı. Bul jerde ol Reyçel attı jas **äyeldi** kezdestiredi jäne ol **medbïke** bolıp jumıs jasadı. Jon öziniñ **dos qızınıñ** kütimimen tez jazılıp ketedi, alayda ol eşqaşan uşa almaytın boladı. Alayda ol basqa adamdardı uşuğa üyretu üşin uşu mektebiniñ **nusqauşısı** boladı. Arada köp uzamay, Réyçel men Jon **erli-zayıptı** atanadı. Olardıñ eki süykimdi balaları boladı, bir ul jäne bir qız. Jïll- nağız änşi. Rok juldızı boluğa umtılğan qızğa bäri de mïkrofonğa aynaladı. Ol burın soñdı siz körmegen eñ süykimdi kişkentay xanşayım. Biraq kişkentay kişi Jonnï **äkesiniñ** izin baspaqşı, öytkeni ol däl **äkesi** sïyaqtı **uşqış** boludı armandaydı. **Äkesi, balası** jäne **nemeresi** tınıq jeksenbi tüsinde uşıp bara jatqan uşaqtardı baqılağandı unatadı. Jon **balasınıñ** bir küni özi sekildi uşaqtardı uşıra alatının biledi. Biraq munday oylar kezinde apat saldarınan qorqınış tuındaydı, alayda ol balasınıñ uşqış bolu umtılısın maqtanış tutadı. Mümkin bir küni ol **äkesiniñ** uşu mektebiniñ **studenti** bolar. Onıñ barlıq jetistikteriniñ işindegi Jonnıñ **januyası-** erekşe maqtan tutatın jetistigi.

4) Parts of the Body
4) Дене мүшелері
4) Dene müşeleri

ankle

тобық

tobıq

---

arm

қол

qol

---

back

арқа

arqa

---

beard

сақал

saqal

---

belly

iш

iş

---

blood

қан

qan

---

body

дене

dene

---

bone

сүйек

süyek

---

brain

ми

mï

---

breast

кеуде

keude

---

buttocks

бөксе

bökse

---

calf

балтыр

baltır

---

cheek

бет

bet

---

chest

төс

tös

---

chin
иек
ïek

ear
құлақ
qulaq

elbow
шынтақ
şıntaq

eye
көз
köz

eyebrow
қас
qas

eyelash
кірпік
kirpik

face
бет
bet

finger
саусақ
sausaq

finger nail

тырнақ

tırnaq

---

fist

жұдырық

judırıq

---

flesh

тән

tän

---

foot/feet

аяқ/аяқтар

ayaq/ayaqtar

---

forearm

қар

qar

---

forehead

маңдай

mañday

---

hair

шаш

şaş

---

hand

қол

qol

---

head

бас

bas

heart

жүрек

jürek

heel

өкше

ökşe

hip

жанбас

janbas

jaw

жақ

jaq

knee

тізе

tize

leg

аяқ

ayaq

lips

ерін

erin

moustache

мұрт

murt

mouth

ауыз

auız

muscle

бұлшықет

bulşıqet

nail

тырнақ

tırnaq

neck

мойын

moyın

nose

мұрын

murın

nostril

танау

tanau

palm

алақан

alaqan

shin

сирақ

sïraq

shoulder

иық

ïıq

skin

тері

teri

spine

омыртқа

omırtqa

stomach

іш

iş

teeth/tooth

тіс/тістер

tis/tister

thigh

сан

san

throat

тамақ

tamaq

thumb

бас бармақ

bas barmaq

---

toe

башай

başay

---

toenail

башай тырна**ғы**

başay tırnağı

---

tongue

тіл

til

---

underarm

қолт**ық**

qoltıq

---

waist

бел

bel

---

wrist

білек

bilek

Related Verbs
Қатысты етістіктер

Qatıstı etistikter

to exercise

жаттығу

jattığu

---

to feel

сезу

sezu

---

to hear

есту

estu

---

to see

көру

köru

---

to smell

иіс шығу

ïis şığu

---

to taste

дәмін тату

dämin tatu

---

to touch

ұстап көру

ustap köru

One day an alien crash landed on planet Earth. He was very confused and didn't know where he was. As he explored this undiscovered world, he happened along a little boy named David. David was eight years old and wasn't scared at all; after all, he knew there were aliens and he was happy to finally meet one. The alien had a large **head** and funny pointing **ears;** and he moved in a curious way with six **legs**! The alien was so confused when he saw the boy, so he asked David, "Why do you look so funny?" David laughed and told him all humans look like this. David has a good **heart** and wanted to make sure the alien was familiar with the people of Earth, so he told him all about how we use our body parts. "Let me tell you all about these funny parts", replied David. "On top of my body is my **head**; we have two **eyes** to see; two **ears** to hear; a **nose** to smell; and a **mouth** to talk and eat." The alien was surprised because he had all of these parts, but they looked much different. "Well then," said the alien, "what are those things you are standing on and why are there only two of them? David said, "These are **legs**, we just put one in front of the other and it makes us walk or run." The alien was amazed that the human could walk with only two **legs,** after all, he had six **legs** and he needed them all to get around! "What are those things that are dangling off your upper **legs**?" asked the alien. "Oh, these? They are called **fingers** and they are attached to my **hands** and **arms**. Look! Aren't they neat? I can wiggle them, tickle with them, I even use them to pick things up. They really come in handy for lots of different things." The alien really wanted a set of those fingers, and then to find out there are **toes** on the end of the **legs**... wow! He just had to have some! The alien wanted to know more, so he continued, "What is that stuff sticking up on the top of your **head**?" David replied, "That is called **hair**. It grows really fast, even after I cut it off, it just grows back out!!

Adult humans have **hair** on other parts of their bodies; l**egs, arms, face,** even their **toes!**" "Why don't you have **hair** on those parts?" asked the alien. David told him that he would not grow **hair** on those parts until he grows up. The alien was satisfied with David's explanation of the human body parts and decided it was time to return home. David was sad to see him go, but so excited to tell his friends all about his encounter with such a curious alien.

Бір күні апат салдарынан басқа ғаламдық келімсек жерге қонады. Ол абыржып, өзінің қайда екенін түсінбейді. Бұндай ашылмаған жерді зерттеп келе жатқанда, Дэвид атты кішкентай баланың қасынан тап болады. Дэвид сегіз жастағы бала еді және ол қорыққан жоқ. Сондай-ақ, келімсектердің болатынын білгендіктен, нәтижесінде ол оны кездестіргеніне қуанды. Келімсектің үлкен **басы** және қызық нүктеленген **құлақтары** болды. Ол өзінің алты **аяғы** арқылы қызықты тәсілмен жүретін. Келімсек баланы көрді де, таң қалды. Және ол баладан: "Неге сіздер сондай қызықты көрінесіздер?"- деп сұрады. Дэвид күлді де, барлық адамдар осылай көрінеді деп жауап берді. Дэвидтің **жүрегі** жұмсақ болғандықтан, келімсектің Жер бетіндегі адамдармен жақсы таныс болуын қалады. Сондықтан, ол келімсекке біздің дене мүшелерімізді қалай пайдаланатынымыз туралы айтып берді. "Бұл қызық мүшелер туралы айтып берейін,"-деді Дэвид. "Менің денемнің төбесінде ол менің **басым**; көру үшін бізде екі **көз** бар; есту үшін екі **құлақ** бар; іискеу үшін **мұрын** бар; және ас ішіп, сөйлеу үшін **ауыз** бар." Келімсек таң қалады, өйткені оның да осындай мүшелері бар, бірақ олар өзгеше болып көрінеді. "Жарайды," деді келімсек, "сені көтеріп тұрған қандай мүшелер және олар неге екеу ғана?" Дэвид:

"Бұл **аяқтар**, біздер бір аяқты екіншісінің алдына қоямыз, осылай жүреміз және жүгіреміз." Келімсек адамдардың екі **аяқпен** ғана жүре білетініне таң қалады, ал оның алты **аяғы** бар және оған қозғалуы үшін олардың барлығы да қажет! "**Аяғыңның** жанында салбырап тұрған қандай мүше?" деп келімсек сұрады. "Бұлар ма? Бұлардың аты **саусақтар** және олар менің **қолыма** жалғасқан. Қара! Сүйкімді көрінбейді ме? Мен оларды қозғай аламын, қыдықтай аламын, мен тіпті олармен заттарды ала аламын. Олар көп жағдайда көмектеседі. Келімсек те осындай саусақатарының болғанын қалады. Кейін ол сондай **башайларды аяғының** басынан көріп қалды. Уау!Онда да осындай саусақтар болуы тиіс! Келімсек әлі де көп зат білгісі келді, сондықтан ол жалғастырды:"**Басыңның** төбесіндегі не нәрсе?" Дэвид: "Оның аты **шаш**, ол тез өседі, тіпті мен оларды қиып тастаған жағдайда да, олар өсіп қайта қалпына келеді. Ересек адамның денесінің басқа жерлерінде де шаш өседі: **аяғында**, **қолында**, **бетінде**, тіпті **башайларында** да!" "Неге сенің сондай дене мүшелеріңе **шаш** өспейді?" деп сұрады келімсек. Дэвид оның есеймегеніше, оның дене мүшелеріне **шаш** өспейтінін айтты. Келімсек Дэвидтің адам дене мүшелерін түсіндіргеніне қанағаттанады және үйіне оралатын уақыт келді деп шешеді. Дэвидтің оның кететініне көңілі түсті, алайда ол мұндай қызыққұмар келімсекті кездестіргені туралы достарына айтуға қобалжып тұрды.

Bir küni apat saldarınan basqa ğalamdıq kelimsek jerge qonadı. Ol abırjıp, öziniñ qayda ekenin tüsinbeydi. Bunday aşılmağan jerdi zerttep kele jatqanda, Dévïd attı kişkentay balanıñ qasınan tap boladı. Dévïd segiz jastağı bala edi jäne ol qorıqqan joq. Sonday-aq, kelimsekterdiñ bolatının bilgendikten, nätïjesinde ol onı kezdestirgenine quandı. Kelimsektiñ ülken **basi** jäne qızıq nüktelengen **qulaqtarı** boldı. Ol öziniñ altı **ayağı** arqılı qızıqtı täsilmen jüretin. Kelimsek balanı kördi de, tañ qaldı. Jäne ol baladan: "Nege sizder sonday qızıqtı körinesizder?"- dep suradı. Dévïd küldi de, barlıq adamdar osılay körinedi dep jauap berdi. Dévïdtiñ **jüregi** jumsaq bolğandıqtan, kelimsektiñ Jer betindegi adamdarmen jaqsı tanıs boluın qaladı. Sondıqtan, ol kelimsekke bizdiñ dene müşelerimizdi qalay paydalanatınımız turalı aytıp berdi. "Bul qızıq müşeler turalı aytıp bereyin,"-dedi Dévïd. "Meniñ denemniñ töbesinde ol meniñ **basım**; köru üşin bizde eki **köz** bar; estu üşin eki **qulaq** bar; iiskeu üşin **murın** bar; jäne as işip, söyleu üşin **auız** bar." Kelimsek tañ qaladı, öytkeni onıñ da osınday müşeleri bar, biraq olar özgeşe bolıp körinedi. "Jaraydı," dedi kelimsek, "seni köterip turğan qanday müşeler jäne olar nege ekeu ğana?" Dévïd: "Bul **ayaqtar**, bizder bir ayaqtı ekinşisiniñ aldına qoyamız, osılay jüremiz jäne jügiremiz." Kelimsek adamdardıñ eki **ayaqpen** ğana jüre biletinine tañ qaladı, al onıñ altı **ayağı** bar jäne oğan qozğaluı üşin olardıñ barlığı da qajet! "**Ayağıñnıñ** janında salbırap turğan qanday müşe?" dep kelimsek suradı. "Bular ma? Bulardıñ atı **sausaqtar** jäne olar meniñ **qolıma** jalğasqan. Qara! Süykimdi körinbeydi me? Men olardı qozğay alamın, qıdıqtay alamın, men tipti olarmen zattardı ala alamın. Olar köp jağdayda kömektesedi. Kelimsek te osınday sausaqatarınıñ bolğanın qaladı. Keyin ol sonday **başaylardı ayağınıñ** basınan körip qaldı. Waw! Onda da osınday sausaqtar boluı tiis! Kelimsek äli de köp zat bilgisi keldi, sondıqtan ol jalğastırdı:"**Basıñnıñ** töbesindegi ne närse?" Dévïd: "Onıñ atı **şaş**, ol tez ösedi, tipti men olardı qiıp tastağan jağdayda da, olar ösip qayta qalpına keledi. Eresek adamnıñ denesiniñ basqa jerlerinde de şaş ösedi: **ayağında, qolında, betinde**, tipti **başaylarında** da!" "Nege seniñ sonday dene müşeleriñe **şaş** öspeydi?" dep suradı kelimsek. Dévïd onıñ eseymegenişe, onıñ dene müşelerine **şaş** öspeytinin ayttı. Kelimsek Dévïdtiñ adam dene müşelerin tüsindirgenine qanağattanadı jäne üyine oralatın waqıt keldi dep şeşedi. Dévïdtiñ onıñ ketetinine köñili tüsti, alayda ol munday qızıqqumar kelimsekti kezdestirgeni turalı dostarına aytuğa qobaljıp turdı.

5) Animals
5) Жануарлар
5) Januarlar

alligator
аллигатор
allïgator

anteater
құмырсқажегі
qumırsqajegi

antelope
бөкен
böken

ape
маймыл
maymıl

armadillo
армадилл
armadïll

baboon
бабуин
babuïn

bat

жарғанат

jarğanat

---

bear

аю

ayu

---

beaver

құндыз

qundız

---

bison

бизон

bïzon

---

bobcat

сілеусін

sileusin

---

camel

түйе

tüye

---

caribou

бұғы

buğı

---

cat

мысық

mısıq

---

chameleon

құбылғы

qubılğı

---

cheetah

қабылан

qabılan

---

chipmunk

боршатышқан

borşatışqan

---

cougar

тауарыстан

tauarıstan

---

cow

сиыр

sиr

---

coyote

койот

koyot

---

crocodile

қолтырауын

qoltırauın

---

deer

марал

maral

---

dinosaur

динзавр

dïnzavr

dog

ит

ït

donkey

есек

esek

elephant

піл

pil

emu

эму түйеқұсы

ému tüyequsı

ferret

күзен

küzen

fox

түлкі

tülki

frog

бақа

baqa

gerbil

сұртышқан

surtışqan

giraffe

керік

kerik

goat

ешкі

eşki

gorilla

горилла

gorilla

groundhog

суыр

suir

guinea pig

теңіз шошқасы

teñiz şoşqası

hamster

атжалман

atjalman

hedgehog

кірпі

kirpi

hippopotamus

гиппопотам

gïppopotam

---

horse

жылқы

jılqı

---

iguana

игуана

ïguana

---

kangaroo

кенгуру

kenguru

---

lemur

лемур

lemur

---

leopard

леопард

leopard

---

lion

арыстан

arıstan

---

lizard

кесіртке

kesirtke

---

llama

таутайлақ

tautaylaq

---

meerkat

сурикат

surïkat

---

mouse/mice

тышқан/тышқандар

tışqan/tışqandar

---

mole

көртышқан

körtışqan

---

monkey

маймыл

maymıl

---

moose

бұлан

bulan

---

mouse

тышқан

tışqan

---

otter

кәмшат

kämşat

---

panda
панда
panda

panther
қабылан
qabılan

pig
доңыз/шошқа
doñız/ şoşqa

platypus
үйректұмсық
üyrektumsıq

polar bear
ақ аю
aq ayu

porcupine
жайра
jayra

rabbit
қоян
qoyan

raccoon
жанат
janat

rat

егеуқұйрық

egeuquyrıq

rhinoceros

мүйізтұмсық

müyiztumsıq

sheep

қой

qoylar

skunk

тарбаған

tarbağan

sloth

ленивец

lenïvec

snake

жылан

jılan

squirrel

тиын

tïın

tiger

жолбарыс

jolbarıs

toad

құрбақа

qurbaqa

turtle

тасбақа

tasbaqa

walrus

сойдақтісті

soydaqtisti

warthog

қабан

qaban

weasel

аққалақ

aqqalaq

wolf

қасқыр

qasqır

zebra

ала құлан

ala qulan

Birds
Құстар

Qustar

canary

шымшық

şımşıq

chicken

балапан

balapan

crow

қарға

qarğa

dove

көгершін

kögerşin

duck

үйрек

üyrek

eagle

бүркіт

bürkit

falcon

сұңқар

suñqar

flamingo

қоқиқаз

qoqïqaz

goose

қаз

qaz

hawk

қаршыға

qarşığa

hummingbird

колибри

kolïbrï

ostrich

түйеқұс

tüyequs

owl

үкі

üki

parrot

тоты

totı

peacock

тауыс

tauıs

pelican

бірқазан

birqazan

---

pheasant

қырғауыл

qırğauıl

---

pigeon

кептер

kepter

---

robin

қызылтамақ шымшық

qızıltamaq şımşıq

---

rooster

әтеш

äteş

---

sparrow

торғай

torğay

---

swan

аққу

aqqu

---

turkey

күркетауық

kürketauıq

Water/Ocean/Beach
Су/Теңіз/Жағалау
Su/Teñiz/Jağalau

bass
алабұға
alabuğa

catfish
лақа
laqa

clam
ұлу
ulu

crab
теңіз шаяны
teñiz şayanı

goldfish
алтын балық
altın balıq

jellyfish
медуза
meduza

lobster
омар
omar

mussel

мидия

mïdïya

oyster

устрица

ustrïca

salmon

албырт

albırt

shark

акула

akula

trout

бахтах

baxtax

tuna

тунец

tunec

whale

кит

kït

Insects
Жәндіктер

Jändikter

ant

құмырсқа

qumırsqa

bee

ара

ara

beetle

қоңыз

qoñız

butterfly

көбелек

köbelek

cockroach

тарақан

taraqan

dragonfly

инелік

ïnelik

earthworm

жер құрты

jer qurtı

flea

бүрге

bürge

fly

шыбын

şıbın

gnat

маса

masa

grasshopper

шегіртке

şegirtke

ladybug

қызыл қоңыз

qızıl qoñız

moth

күйе

küye

mosquito

маса

masa

spider

өрмекші

örmekşi

wasp

сона

sona

Related Verbs
Қатысты етістіктер
Qatıstı etistikter

to eat

жеу

Jeu

---

to bark

үру

üru

---

to chase

аңду

añdu

---

to feed

тамақтандыру

tamaqtandıru

---

to hibernate

қыстау

qıstau

---

to hunt

аң аулау

añ aulau

---

to move

қозғалу

qozǧalu

to perch

дүңкию/үйілу

düñkïyu/üyilu

to prey

аң аулау

añ aulau

to run

жүгіру

jügiru

to swim

жүзу

jüzu

to wag

шайқау

şayqau

to walk

жүру

jüru

Sarah is a seven year old girl who loves to visit the zoo. Her mom takes her to the local zoo at least once a week to see her favorite animals. This is an account of her usual visit to the zoo:

When they arrive, they must pass by the **flamingos** and boy do they smell! They are pretty to look at, but don't get too close! Sarah insists that they visit her favorite animal first, the **elephants**. She loves how big, yet gentle they are. They spend time watching the **elephants** move about their habitat and one time, she even got to see an **elephant** paint! Next, they visit the Birds' Nest exhibit. They have many different species of **birds** on display, including **sparrows**, **robins**, **peacocks**, **canaries**, **hummingbirds**, they even have an **eagle**! The **eagle** is so majestic; it is Sarah's favorite **bird**. Sometimes the **eagle**'s trainer will put on a show and Sarah just loves to see it spread its wings! After visiting the birds, Sarah likes to visit the mammal section of the zoo. They have **bears**, **tigers**, **lions**, **monkeys**, they even have **pandas**! One of the **pandas** had twin babies last year and Sarah has really enjoyed watching them grow up. After lunch, they visit the **reptile** house; there are lots of scaly looking animals there! The **alligators** are big and scary, but Sarah likes to watch from a distance. They also have **frogs** in lots of different colors; some are green, some are yellow and black, and some are blue! The best animals in the **reptile** house are the **snakes**. Some are stretched out long and some are coiled up taking a nap! They come in many different colors as well. Did you know that **snakes** eat **mice**? Sarah once got to see a **snake** eat its lunch, it was a little yucky to watch, but neat to see how a **snake** eats. After visiting the **reptiles**, Sarah and her mom go to see the **meerkats** and **warthogs**. They always make Sarah think of her favorite movie characters. The **meerkats** are silly little creatures and the **warthogs** just lay around in the mud all day! Sarah then goes to visit the tallest animal in the zoo, the **giraffe**. One day she even got to feed one! Its mouth is very weird to touch and it has a long tongue. One of the more popular sites at the zoo is the petting zoo. Sarah gets to brush the coat of **goats**, **sheep**, and even **pigs**! One last stop, to ride the train. While on the zoo train, Sarah gets to see lots of different animals, such as **kangaroos**, **ostriches**, **turtles**, and many more! Maybe one day, Sarah's mom can talk her into going to the aquarium instead of the zoo. Sarah would surely enjoy seeing **sharks**, **whales**, and **jellyfish**!

Сара хайуанаттар бағына барғанды ұнататын жеті жасар қыз. Оның анасы оны жергілікті хайуанаттар бағына кемінде аптасына бір рет оның сүйікті жануарларын көруге алып барады. Оның әдеттегі хайуанаттар бағына бару жоспары: Олар келген кезде **қоқиқаздарға** баруы міндетті және олардан жағымсыз иіс шығады. Оларды бақылаған тамаша, бірақ жақындауға болмайды! Сара ең бірінші оның сүйікті жануары **пілдерге** баруды талап етеді. Ол **пілдердің** сондай үлкен, бірақ нәзік болатынын ұнатады. Олар **пілдердің** өмір сүру ортасында қозғалысын бақылау үшін уақыт жұмсайды және бір күні ол тіпті **пілдің** сурет салғанын көре алды. Келесі, олар Құстар Ұясы Көрмесіне барды. Мұнда көрсетілетін әртүрлі құстар бар: **торғайлар**, **қызылтамақ шымшықтар**, **тауыстар**, **шымшықтар**, **колибрилер**, тіпті оларда **бүркіт** те бар! Бүркіт сондай ғажайып; Ол Сараның сүйікті құсы. Кейде **бүркіттің** жаттықтырушысы шоу көрсетеді, Сара сол кезде **бүркіттің** қанатын жайғанын көргенді ұнатады. Құстарды бақылап болған соң, ол хайуанаттар бағындағы сүтқоректілер бөлімшесіне барғанды ұнатады. Мұнда **аюлар**, **жолбарыстар**, **арыстандар**, **маймылдар**, тіпті мұнда **пандалар** да бар! **Пандалардың** бірі былтыр егіз қонжықтар тапты және Сара олардың өсіп келе жатқанын бақылағанды ұнатады. Түстен кейін, олар **рептилия** үйіне барады. Бұл жерде қабыршақпен қапталған жануарлар көп. **Аллигаторлар** үлкен және қорқынышты, бірақ Сара оларды алыстан бақылағанды ұнатады. Мұнда сонымен қатар, түрлі түсті **бақалар** бар. Кейбіреулері жасыл, кейбіреулері сары және қара, және кейбіреулері көк. **Рептилия** үйіндегі ең күшті жануарлар – **жыландар**. Кейбіреулері ұзыннан созылып жатса, кейбіреулері дөңгеленіп алып, ұйқыға кетуде! Олардың да көптеген түстері бар. **Жыландардың тышқандарды** жейтінін білесіз бе? Бір күні Сара **жыланның тышқан** жеп жатқанын көрді, оған қарауға жағымсыз болды, бірақ **жылан** оны ұқыпты жеді. **Рептилияларға** барғаннан кейін, Сара және оның анасы **қабандар** мен **сурикаттарды** көруге барады. Оларды көргенде Сара өзінің сүйікті фильм кейіпкерлерін есіне түсіреді. **Сурикаттар** –кішкентай аңқау жануарлар және **қабандар** күні бойы лай үстінде жатады! Содан Сара хайуанаттар бағындағы ең ұзын жануарға барады, ол- **керік**. Бір күні Сара оны тіпті тамақтандырып көрді. Оның аузын ұстап көрген қызық және оның ұзын тілі бар. хайуанаттар бағының ең танымал бөлігі –үй жануарларының бағы. Сара **ешкілердің**, **қойлардың** және тіпті **шошқалардың** жүнін тарап көрді. Поезға отыру- соңғы аялдама. Хайуанаттар бағындағы поезбен Сара **кенгурулар**, **түйеқұстар** мен **тасбақалар** сияқты көптеген жануарларды көруге барады! Мүмкін бір күні Сараның анасы оған хайуанаттар бағының орнына аквариумға баруды ұсынар. Сара **акулалар**, **киттер** мен **медузаларға** қарауды ұнатар еді.

Sara xayuanattar bağına barğandı unatatın jeti jasar qız. Onıñ anası onı jergilikti xayuanattar bağına keminde aptasına bir ret onıñ süyikti januarların köruge alıp baradı. Onıñ ädettegi xayuanattar bağına baru josparı: Olar kelgen kezde **qoqïqazdarğa** baruı mindetti jäne olardan jağımsız iis şığadı. Olardı baqılağan tamaşa, biraq jaqındauğa bolmaydı! Sara eñ birinşi onıñ süyikti januarı **pilderge** barudı talap etedi. Ol **pilderdiñ** sonday ülken, biraq näzik bolatının unatadı. Olar **pilderdiñ** ömir süru ortasında qozğalısın baqılau üşin köp waqıt jumsaydı jäne bir küni ol tipti **pildiñ** suret salğanın köre aldı. Kelesi, olar Qustar Uyasy Körmesine bardı. Munda körsetiletin ärtürli qustar bar: **torğaylar, qızıltamaq şımşıqtar, tauıstar, şımşıqtar, kolïbrïler,** tipti olarda **bürkit** te bar! **Bürkit** sonday ğajayıp; Ol Saranıñ süyikti qusı. Keyde **bürkittiñ** jattıqtıruşısı şou körsetedi, Sara sol kezde **bürkittiñ** qanatın jayğanın körgendi unatadı. Qustardı baqılap bolğan soñ, ol xayuanattar bağındağı sütqorektiler bölimşesine barğandı unatadı. Munda **ayular, jolbarıstar, arıstandar, maymıldar,** tipti munda **pandalar** da bar! **Pandalardıñ** biri bıltır egiz qonjıqtar taptı jäne Sara olardıñ ösip kele jatqanın baqılağandı unatadı. Tüsten keyin, olar **reptïlïya** üyine baradı. Bul jerde qabırşaqpen qaptalğan januarlar köp. **Allïgatorlar** ülken jäne qorqınıştı, biraq Sara olardı alıstan baqılağandı unatadı. Munda sonımen qatar, türli tüsti **baqalar** bar. Keybireuleri jasıl, keybireuleri sarı jäne qara, jäne keybireuleri kök. **Reptïlïya** üyindegi eñ küşti januarlar – **jılandar.** Keybireuleri uzınnan sozılıp jatsa, keybireuleri döñgelenip alıp, uyqığa ketude! Olardıñ da köptegen tüsteri bar. **Jılandardıñ tışqandardy** jeytinin bilesiz be? Bir küni Sara jılannıñ tışqan jep jatqanın kördi, oğan qarauğa jağımsız boldı, biraq **jılan** onı uqıptı jedi. **Reptïlïyalarğa** barğannan keyin, Sara jäne onıñ anası **qabandar** men **surïkattardı** köruge barady. Olardı körgende Sara öziniñ süyikti fïl'm keyipkerlerin esine tüsiredi. **Surïkattar** –kişkentay añqau januarlar jäne **qabandar** küni boyı lay üstinde jatadı! Sodan Sara xayuanattar bağındağı eñ uzın januarğa baradı, ol- **kerik**. Bir küni Sara onı tipti tamaqtandırıp kördi. Onıñ auzın ustap körgen qızıq jäne onıñ uzın tili bar. xayuanattar bağınıñ eñ tanımal böligi –üy januarlarınıñ bağı. Sara **eşkilerdiñ**, **qoylardıñ** jäne tipti **şoşqalardıñ** jünin tarap kördi. Poezğa otıru- soñğı ayaldama. Xayuanattar bağındağı poezben Sara kengurular, tüyequstar men tasbaqalar sïyaqtı köptegen januarlardı köruge baradı! Mümkin bir küni Saranıñ anası oğan xayuanattar bağınıñ ornına akvarïumğa barudı usınar. Sara akulalar, kïtter men meduzalarğa q/qaraudı unatar edi.

6) Plants and Trees
6) Өсімдіктер мен талдар
6) Ösimdikter men taldar

acacia

қараған

qarağan

acorn

емен жаңғағы

emen jañğağı

annual

бір жылдық өсімдік

bir jıldıq ösimdik

apple tree

алма ағашы

alma ağaşı

bamboo

бамбук

bambuk

bark

қабық

qabıq

bean

ірі бұршақ

iri burşaq

---

berry

жидек

jïdek

---

birch

қайың

qayıñ

---

blossom

гүлдену

güldenu

---

branch

бұтақ

butaq

---

brush

бұта

buta

---

bud

бүршік

bürşik

---

bulb

пиязшық

pïyazşıq

---

bush
бұта
buta

cabbage
қырыққабат
qırıqqabat

cactus
кактус
kaktus

carnation
қалампыр
qalampır

cedar
балқарағай
balqarağay

cherry tree
шие ағашы
şïe ağaşı

chestnut
талшын
talşın

corn
жүгері
jügeri

cypress

сауырағаш

sauırağaş

deciduous

жапырақты

japıraqtı

dogwood

қызыл тал

qızıl tal

eucalyptus

эвкалипт

évkalïpt

evergreen

мәңгі жасыл

mäñgi jasıl

fern

қырыққұлақ

qırıqqulaq

fertilizer

тыңайтқыш

tıñaytqış

fir

шырша

şırşa

flower

гүл

gül

foliage

жапырақтар

japıraqtar

forest

орман

orman

fruit

жеміс

jemis

garden

бақша

baqşa

ginko

гинкго

gïnkgo

grain

дән

dän

grass

шөп

şöp

hay

пішен

pişen

---

herb

шөп

şöp

---

hickory

гикори

gïkorï

---

ivy

шырмауық

şırmauıq

---

juniper

арша

arşa

---

kudzu

кудзу

kudzu

---

leaf/leaves

жапырақ/жапырақтар

japıraq/japıraqtar

---

lettuce

салат

салат

---

lily

лалагүл

lalagül

---

magnolia

магнолия

magnolïya

---

maple tree

үйеңкі

üyeñki

---

moss

мүк

mük

---

nut

жаңғақ

jañğaq

---

oak

емен

emen

---

palm tree

пальма ағашы

pal'ma ağaşı

---

pine cone

қарағай бүршігі

qarağay bürşigi

pine tree

қарағай

qarağay

plant

көшет

köşet

peach tree

шабдалы ағашы

şabdalı ağaşı

pear tree

алмұрт ағашы

almurt ağaşı

petal

гүл күлте

gül külte

poison ivy

улы шырмауық

ulı şırmawıq

pollen

гүл аталығы

gül atalığı

pumpkin

асқабақ

asqabaq

root

тамыр

tamır

---

roses

раушан гүлдер

rauşan gülder

---

sage

жалбыз

jalbız

---

sap

шырын

şırın

---

seed

тұқым

tuqım

---

shrub

түп

tüp

---

squash

кәді

kädi

---

soil

топырақ

topıraq

---

stem

сабақ

sabaq

thorn

тікенек

tikenek

tree

ағаш/тал

ağaş/tal

trunk

діңгек

diñgek

vegetable

көкөніс

kökönis

vine

жүзім шағы

jüzim şağı

weed

арамшөп

aramşöp

Related Verbs
Қатысты етістіктер
Qatıstı etistikter

to fertilize
тыңайту
tıñaytu

to gather
жинау
jïnau

to grow
өсіру
ösiru

to harvest
астық жинау
astıq jïnau

to pick
жинау
jïnau

to plant
көшет отырғызу
köşet otırğızu

to plow
жер жырту
jer jırtu

to rake

қопсыту

qopsıtu

---

to sow

шашу

şaşu

---

to spray

тозаңдату

tozañdatu

---

to water

суару

suaru

---

to weed

отау

otau

Farmer Smith was a kind old man. He ran the local farm and orchard. One day, while out harvesting **corn**, a bird hobbled over and sat down beside him. Farmer Smith noticed the poor little bird had a broken wing, so he gathered up his supplies and cradled the bird in one of his baskets. The bird could not fly and was helpless, so Farmer Smith decided to nurse the bird back to good health. He used a small piece of **bark** to bandage the broken wing. Every day Farmer Smith would take the bird for a walk and they would rest against the **trunk** of an old **oak tree** at the edge of the property. The farmer loved to tell the bird all about the different **plants** on his farm. He told of the

pine trees that lined his property. These **trees** were perfect Christmas **trees**. He told of the **flowers** that grew wild near the lake, he explained how they started as a seed, and then grew into a bulb, then eventually into a beautiful **flower**. They were so colorful and vibrant; they remind the farmer of his wife. He would bring her **roses** every day for her to use on the dinner table. His wife was a wonderful cook, she could cook anything that the farmer grew; **squash, pumpkin, pears, apples, cabbage,** and many more. The way she used the **herbs** was like magic! The little bird loved to hear the stories about the farmer's wife, just hearing about her brought the bird comfort. One day, while the farmer was out **tilling** the **soil,** he heard a small sound approaching him; he turned around to see it was the little bird he had been caring for. She had learned to fly again! The farmer decided it was time for the bird to go live in the **forest** again. She was strong enough and prepared to survive on her own. It was a sad day, but the farmer took the bird into the **deciduous forest** and released her. One day, in early spring the farmer noticed a bird on his window sill. He couldn't believe his eyes, it was the same bird. He was so pleased to see the bird again, for it reminded him of his wife. Now, every spring, the bird comes to visit the farmer. He and the bird go to that old **oak tree** and Farmer Smith tells a new story about his wife. I don't know whatever happened to that bird, but it visited the farmer every year until the farmer passed away. It even visited his window sill at the hospital the year before he died. No one has ever seen it happen, but I know that the bird brings a single **rose** to Farmer Brown's resting site. Some may see the bird as a small, helpless creature, but for Farmer Smith, the bird helped to fill a void for his remaining years.

Фермер Смит мырза қарт адам еді. Оның жергілікті фермасы мен бағы болды. Бір күні ол **бидай** жинап жатқан кезде бір құс ақсаңдап, оның қасына келіп отырды. Фермер Смит оның қанаты сынық екенін байқап, себет ішіне жинаған егіннің үстіне қойып, бесіктей шайқайды. Құс өздігінен ұша алмады және әлсіз болды, сондықтан фермер Смит оның денсаулығын қайтадан қапына келтіруді шешті. Ол құстың сынған қанатын байлау үшін **ағаш қабығын** пайдаланды. Күнде фермер Смит құсты алып, серуендеуге шығаратын және өз меншігінің шетіндегі **ескі еменнің діңгегіне** қарсы демалып жататын. Фермер Смит құсқа өзінің фермасындағы әртүрлі **көшеттер** туралы барлығын айтқанды ұнататын. Ол меншігін қоршап тұрған **қарағай талдары** туралы айтты. Бұл **талдар** әмбебап Жаңа Жыл **шыршыларын** болатын. Ол өзен жанындағы жабайы өскен **гүлдер** туралы да айтып берді, ол олардың қалай бірінші тұқымнан басталғанын, кейін пиязшық болып өскенін, содан соң тамаша әдемі **гүлдерге** айналғанын түсіндірді. Олардың алуан түрлі түстері мен жарқырағандығы оған оның зайыбын есіне салатын. Ол оның **раушан гүлдерін** күнде оған түскі ас үстеліне қою үшін алып келетін еді. Оның зайыбы керемет аспазшы болатын, ол фермер өсіретін барлық заттан ас әзірлей алатын: **кәділер**, **асқабақтар**, **алмалар** және **қырыққабаттар** және тағы басқа. Оның шөптерді пайдалануы бір ғажайып болатын. Кішкентай құсқа фермердің зайыбы туралы әңгімелерді тыңдаған ұнайды, тек ол туралы тыңдағанның өзі құсты жайлы сезіндіретін. Бір күні фермер Смит **жерді өңдеп** жатқан кезде оған жақындап келе жатқан дауысты естіді, ол бұрылып қараса, өзінің күтім жасап жүрген құсын көреді. Ол қайтадан ұшуды үйреніп жүр екен! Фермер құсты **орманға** бостандыққа жіберетін уақыт келді деген шешімге келеді.Ол қажетті күшін жинап, өздігінен өмір сүруге талпынып жатыр. Бұл көңілсіз күн болатын, бірақ фермер құсты алып, **жапырақты орманға** босатып жібереді. Бір күні, ерте көктемде ол терезе алды тақтайшасында бір құс тұрғанын байқайды. Оның алдында дәл сол таныс құсы тұрғанына ол өз көзіне сене алмайды. Ол құсты көргеніне сондай қуанады, өйткені құс оның зайыбын есіне түсіретін. Ендігі, құс әр көктемде фермерге келіп тұратын. Ол және құс **ескі емен** ағашының түбіне барып, фермер Смит өзінің зайыбы туралы жаңа бір әңгіме айтып беретін. Бұл құсқа не болғанын білмеймін, бірақ ол фермер қаза болғанға дейін жыл сайын келіп тұратын. Ол тіптен фермердің қаза болғанынан бір жыл бұрын аурухана терезесінің алдындағы тақтайшаға келіп тұрды. Бұны ешкім де көрген емес, бірақ мен бұл құстың фермер Браунның демалатын жеріне жалғыз **раушан** әкелгенін білемін. Кейбір адамдар құсты әлсіз, кішкентай жануардай көруі мүмкін, алайда бұл құс фермер Смиттің соңғы жылдарындағы өмірін мағынаға толтырды.

Fermer Smït mırza qart adam edi. Onıñ jergilikti fermasy men bağı boldı. Bir küni ol **bïday** jïnap jatqan kezde bir qus aqsañdap, onıñ qasına kelip otırdı. Fermer Smït onıñ qanatı sınıq ekenin bayqap, sebet işine jïnağan eginniñ üstine qoyıp, besiktey şayqaydı. Qus özdiginen uşa almadı jäne älsiz boldı, sondıqtan fermer Smït onıñ densaulığın qaytadan qapına keltirudi şeşti. Ol qustıñ sınğan qanatın baylau üşin **ağaş qabığın** paydalandı. Künde fermer Smït qustı alıp, seruendeuge şığaratın jäne öz menşiginiñ şetindegi **eski emenniñ diñgegine** qarsı demalıp jatatın. Fermer Smït qusqa öziniñ fermasındağı ärtürli **köşetter** turalı barlığın aytqandı unatatın. Ol menşigin qorşap turğan **qarağay taldarı** tualı ayttı. Bul **taldar** ämbebap Jaña Jıl **şırşıların** bolatın. Ol özen janındağı jabayı ösken **gülder** turalı da aytıp berdi, ol olardıñ qalay birinşi tuqımnan bastalğanın, keyin pïyazşıq bolıp öskenin, sodan soñ tamaşa ädemi **gülderge** aynalğanın tüsindirdi. Olardıñ aluan türli tüsteri men jarqırağandığı oğan onıñ zayıbın esine salatın. Ol onıñ **rauşan gülderin** künde oğan tüski as üsteline qoyu üşin alıp keletin edi. Onıñ zayıbı keremet aspazşı bolatın, ol fermer ösiretin barlıq zattan as äzirley alatın: **kädiler, asqabaqtar, almalar** jäne **qırıqqabattar** jäne tağı basqa. Onıñ şöpterdi paydalanuı bir ğajayıp bolatın. Kişkentay qusqa fermerdiñ zayıbı turalı äñgimelerdi tıñdağan unaydı, tek ol turalı tıñdağannıñ özi qustı jaylı sezindiretin. Bir küni fermer Smït **jerdi öñdep** jatqan kezde oğan jaqındap kele jatqan dauıstı estïdi, ol burılıp qarasa, öziniñ kütim jasap jürgen qusın köredi. Ol qaytadan uşudı üyrenip jür eken! Fermer qustı **ormanğa** bostandıqqa jiberetin waqıt keldi degen şeşimge keledi.Ol qajetti küşin jïnap, özdiginen ömir süruge talpınıp jatır. Bul köñilsiz kün bolatın, biraq fermer qustı alıp, **japıraqtı ormanğa** bosatıp jiberedi. Bir küni, erte köktemde ol tereze aldı taqtayşasında bir qus turğanın bayqaydı. Onıñ aldında däl sol tanıs qusı turğanına ol öz közine sene almaydı. Ol qustı körgenine sonday quanadı, öytkeni qus onıñ zayıbın esine tüsiretin. Endigi, qus är köktemde fermerge kelip turatın. Ol jäne qus **eski emen** ağaşınıñ tübine barıp, fermer Smït öziniñ zayıbı turalı jaña bir äñgime aytıp beretin. Bul qusqa ne bolğanın bilmeymin, biraq ol fermer qaza bolğanğa deyin jıl sayın kelip turatın. Ol tïpten fermerdiñ qaza bolğanınan bir jıl burın auruxana terezesiniñ aldındağı taqtayşağa kelip turdı. Bunı eşkim de körgen emes, biraq men bul qustıñ fermer Braunnıñ demalatın jerine jalğız **rauşan** äkelgenin bilemin. Keybir adamdar qustı älsiz, kişkentay januarday körwi mümkin, alayda bul qus fermer Smïttiñ soñğı jıldarındağı ömirin mağınağa toltırdı.

7) Greetings/Introductions:
7) Сәлемдесу/Таныстыру
7) Sälemdesu/Tanıstıru

Good morning
Қайырлы таң
Qayırlı tañ

Good afternoon
Қайырлы күн
Qayırlı kün

Good evening
Қайырлы кеш
Qayırlı keş

Good night
Қайырлы түн
Qayırlı tün

Hi
Сәлем
Sälem

Hello
Сәлеметсіз бе?
Sälemetsiz be?

Have you met (name)?

Сіз (аты)таны**с**сыз б**а**?

Siz (atı)tanıssız ba?

Haven't we met?

Біз тан**ы**с емеспіз б**е**?

Biz tanıs emespiz be?

How are you?

Қалайс**ы**з?

Qalaysız?

How are you today?

Бүгін қалы**ң**ыз қалай?

Bügin qalıñız qalay?

How do you do?

Қ**а**л жағдайы**ң**ыз қалай?

Qal jağdayıñız qalay?

How's it going?

Қалай жағдай?

Qalay jağday?

I am (name)

М**е**н (аты)

Men (atı)

I don't think we've met.

Б**ұр**ын кездестік деп ойламаймын

Burın kezdestik dep oylamaymın

It's nice to meet you.

Танысқаныма қуаныштымын

Tanısqanıma quanıştımın

Meet (name)

Танысып қойыңыз (аты)

Tanısıp qoyıñız (atı)

My friends call me (nickname)

Менің достарым мені (жалған аты) деп атайды

Meniñ dostarım meni (jalğan atı) dep ataydı

My name is (name)

Менің атым (аты)

Meniñ atım (atı)

Nice to meet you

Танысқаныма қуаныштымын

Tanısqanıma quanıştımın

Nice to see you again.

Қайта көріскеніме қуаныштымын

Qayta köriskenime quanıştımın

Pleased to meet you.

Танысқаныма қуаныштымын

Tanısqanıma quanıştımın

This is (name)

Бұл (аты)

Bul (atı)

What's your name?

Сіздің атыңыз кім?

Sizdiñ atıñız kim?

Who are you?

Сіз кімсіз?

Siz kimsiz?

Greeting Answers
Сәлемдесу жауаптары

Sälemdesu jauaptarı

Fine, thanks

Тамаша, рахмет

Tamaşa, raxmet

I'm exhausted

Мен әлсіредім

Men älsiredim

I'm okay

Жақсымын

Jaqsımın

I'm sick

Мен ауырып тұрмын

Men auırıp turmın

I'm tired

Мен шаршадым

Men şarşadım

Not too bad

Жаман емес

Jaman emes

Not too well, actually

Шын мәнінде, жақсы емес

Şın mäninde, jaqsı emes

Very well

Өте жақсы

Öte jaqsı

Saying Goodbye
Қоштасу

Qoştasu

Bye

Сау бол

Sau bol

Good bye

Сау бол

Sau bol

Good night

Қайырлы түн

Qayırlı tün

See you

Көріскенше

Köriskenşe

See you later

Кейін керіскенше

Keyin keriskenşe

See you next week

Келесі аптада көріскенше

Kelesi aptada köriskenşe

See you soon

Жақын арада көріскенше

Jaqın arada köriskenşe

See you tomorrow

Ертең көріскенше

Erteñ köriskenşe

Courtesy
Сыпайылық

Sıpayılıq

Excuse me

Кешіріңіз

Keşiriñiz

Pardon me

Кешіріңіз

Keşiriñiz

I'm sorry

Кешіріңіз

Keşiriñiz

Thanks

Рахмет

Raxmet

Thank you

Рахмет сізге

Raxmet sizge

You're welcome

Оқасы жоқ

Oqası joq

Congratulations

Құттықтаулар

Quttıqtaular

Get well soon

Жазылып кетіңіз

Jazılıp ketiñiz

Good luck

Сәттілік тілеймін

Sättilik tileimin

Happy New Year

Жаңа жылыңызбен

Jaña Jılıñızben

Happy Easter

Пасха мейрамымен

Pasxa meyramımen

Merry Christmas

Рождество құтты болсын

Rojdestvo quttı bolsın

Well done

Жарайсың

Jaraysıñ

Related Verbs
Қатысты етістіктер

Qatıstı etistikter

---

to greet

сәлемдесу

sälemdesu

---

to meet

танысу/кездесу

tanısu/kezdesu

---

to say

айту

Aytu

---

to shake hands

қол алысу

qol alısu

---

to talk

сөйлесу

söylesu

---

to thank

рахмет айту

raxmet aytu

This is the story of a man named Pop. He just started a new job as a greeter at the local discount store. His son was so proud, he gave him a card that said, "**Congratulations**". He is a little nervous because he has never been a store greeter before. Throughout the day, there are so many customers going in and out of the store, sometimes Pop forgets what he should say. "**Pleased to meet you**" or "**Can I help you out?**" are good options for being polite. His manager assured him, saying, "You will be just fine, so don't worry." He begins the work day with a smile on his face, but by the end of the day, his smile is erased. "**Good morning**," he says with a smile to the nice lady walking down the produce aisle. "**How are you doing?**" asked Pop, but she must not have heard him, because she didn't stop to say **hello**. "Hmm", said Pop, I guess she didn't hear me because a polite person would have said something like, '**Fine, how are you?**' or '**I'm fine, thank you.**' Next there was man with a bushy white beard, he looked very friendly and kind. Pop greeted him politely and said, "**Happy New Year!**" The man just grunted and went on his way, I guess he wasn't friendly after all. Pop replied, "**Have a good day!**" The next several customers were polite and spoke to him. Some of the customers said, "**How do you do?**" and one said, "**My name is Jim. What is your name?**" As the day went on, Pop got really tired and his **greetings** were losing not seeming as effective as earlier in the day. His manager was upset, but gave him another chance. He warned Pop that just saying "**Hi**" or "**Hello**" wasn't enough for the friendly environment our customers are used to. "If you want to make a good impression, you have to be polite. You can say something like, '**Merry Christmas**' or '**Good day to you, sir**', but please be nice to everyone you meet. Finally, as the end of the day was nearing, Pop was very happy to finally be able to say, "**Good night**." He went home without his smile, but said tomorrow is a new day and I will make sure to smile for everyone.

Бұл Поп атты ер адамның оқиғасы. Ол жақын арада жергілікті дисконттық дүкеннің қарсы алғышы болып жаңа жұмысқа орналасты. Оны ұлы сондай мақтан тұтатын, ол оған "**Құттықтаймын**" деп жазылған ашық хат сыйлады. Ол аздап қобалжып тұрды, өйткені ол бұрын дүкен қарсы алғышы болып көрмеген еді. Күні бойы көптеген сатып алушылар дүкенге кіріп – шығып жатты, кейде Поп не айту керектігін ұмытып қалатын. "**Танысқаныма қуаныштымын**" немесе "**Сізге көмектесейін бе**?" сөздері сыпайы болуға, мүмкіндік береді. Оның менеджері "Сіз жақсы жұмыс жасайтын боласыз, сондықтан қобалжымаңыз," деп сендірді. Ол жұмысын күлімсіреп бастайды, бірақ жұмыс аяғында оның күлімсіреуінің ізі де қалмайды. "**Қайырлы таң**,"- деді ол өнімдердің жанынан өтіп бара жатқан сүйкімді ханымға. "**Қал жағдайыңыз қалай**?"- деп сұрады Поп, бірақ ол естімеген болар, өйткені ол сәлемдесу үшін тоқтаған жоқ. "Хмм",- деді Поп, Ол мені естімеген шығар, өйткені сыпайы адам '**Жақсы, өзініңіз қалайсыз**?' немесе '**Мен жақсымын, рахмет**' секілді жауап беруі тиіс қой. Кейін сақалды қалың әрі ақ ер адам кірді, ол өте досшыл және мейірімді болып көрінді. Поп оны сыпайлы қарсы алып, "**Жаңа Жылыңызбен**!" деді. Ол адам бұрқылдады да, өз жолымен кете берді. Ол түбінде мүмкін мырза адам емес шығар деп ойлаймын. Поп "**Күніңіз жақсы өтсін!**" деп жауап берді. Келесі бірнеше сатып алушылар онымен сыпайы болды және онымен сөйлесті. Кейбір сатып алушылар"**Қалайсыз?**" деді, олардың біреуі "**Менің атым Джим. Сіздің атыңыз кім?**" - деп сұрады. Күннің ұзай беруімен, Поп шынайы шаршады және оның **сәлемдесуі** басындағыдай әсерлі болмады. Оның менеджері қапаланды, бірақ оған тағы бір мүмкіндік берді. Оның ескертуі бойынша Поптың жай "**Салем**" немесе "**Сәлеметсіз бе?**" деуі біздің сатып алушыларымыздың үйренген жақсы шырайлы ортаға жеткіліксіз."Егер сен жақсы әсер қалдырғың келсе, сен сыпайлы болуға тиіссің. "**Рождество құтты болсын**" немесе "**Көріскенше күн жақсы болсын, мырза,**" деуіңе болады, бірақ сен әрбір кездескен адамға сыпайылық көрсетуіңді сұраймын. Нәтижесінде кеш жақындаған кезде Поп "**Қайырлы түн**" деп айта алатынына қуанды. Ол үйіiне күлімсіреусіз кетті, бірақ ертең жаңа күн басталады және мен әрбір адамға күлімсірей алатын боламын деп шешті.

Bul Pop attı er adamnıñ oqiğası. Ol jaqın arada jergilikti diskonttıq dükenniñ qarsı alğışı bolıp jaña jumısqa ornalastı. Onı ulı sonday maqtan tutatın, ol oğan "**Quttıqtaymın**" dep jazılğan aşıq xat sıyladı. Ol azdap qobaljıp turdı, öytkeni ol burın düken qarsı alğışı bolıp körmegen edi. Küni boyı köptegen satıp aluşılar dükenge kirip – şığıp jattı, keyde Pop ne aytu kerektigin umıtıp qalatın. "**Tanısqanıma quanıştımın**" nemese "**Sizge kömekteseyin be?**" sözderi sıpayı boluğa mümkindik beredi. Onıñ menedjeri "Siz jaqsı jumıs jasaytın bolasız, sondıqtan qobaljımañız," dep sendirdi. Ol jumısın külimsirep bastaydı, biraq jumıs ayağında onıñ külimsireuiniñ izi de qalmaydı. "**Qayırlı tañ**,"- dedi ol önimderdiñ janınan ötip bara jatqan süykimdi xanımğa. "**Qal jağdayıñız qalay?**"- dep suradı Pop, biraq ol estimegen bolar, öytkeni ol sälemdesu üşin toqtağan joq. "Xmm",- dedi Pop, Ol meni estimegen şığar, öytkeni sıpayı adam '**Jaqsı, öziniñiz qalaysız?**' nemese '**Men jaqsımın, raxmet**' sekildi jauap berui tiis qoy. Keyin saqaldı qalıñ äri aq er adam kirdi, ol öte dosşıl jäne meyirimdi bolıp körindi. Pop onı sıpaylı qarsı alıp, "**Jaña Jılıñızben!**" dedi. Ol adam burqıldadı da, öz jolımen kete berdi. Ol tübinde mümkin mırza adam emes şığar dep oylaymın. Pop " **Küniñiz jaqsı ötsin!**" dep jawap berdi. Kelesi birneşe satıp aluşılar onımen sıpayı boldı jäne onımen söylesti. Keybir satıp aluşılar "**Qalaysız?**" dedi, olardıñ bireui "**Meniñ atım Jim. Sizdiñ atıñız kim?**" - dep suradı. Künniñ uzay beruimen, Pop şınayı şarşadı jäne onıñ **sälemdesui** basındağıday äserli bolmadı. Onıñ menedjeri qapalandı, biraq oğan tağı bir mümkindik berdi. Onıñ eskertui boyınşa Poptıñ jay "**Salem**" nemese "**Sälemetsiz be?**" deui bizdiñ satıp aluşılarımızdıñ üyrengen jaqsı şıraylı ortağa jetkiliksiz."Eger sen jaqsı äser qaldırğıñ kelse, sen sıpaylı boluğa tiissiñ. "**Rojdestvo quttı bolsın**" nemese "**Köriskenşe kün jaqsı bolsın, mırza,**" deuiñe boladı, biraq sen ärbir kezdesken adamğa sıpayılıq körsetuiñdi suraymın. Nätijesinde keş jaqındağan kezde Pop "**Qayırlı tün**" dep ayta alatınına quandı. Ol üyine külimsireusiz ketti, biraq erteñ jaña kün bastaladı jäne men ärbir adamğa külimsirey alatın bolamın dep şeşti.

8) House
8) Үй
8) Üy

air conditioner

ауа салқындатқышы

awa salqındatqışı

---

appliances

техника

texnïka

---

attic

шатыр

şatır

---

awning

бастырма

bastırma

---

backyard

артқы аула

artqı aula

---

balcony

балкон

balkon

---

basement

жертөле

jertöle

bathroom

ванна бөлмесі

vanna bölmesi

bath tub

ванна

vanna

bed

кереует

kereuet

bedroom

ұйықтайтын бөлме

uyıqtaytın bölme

blanket

көрпе

körpe

blender

блендер

blender

blinds

перде

perde

bookshelf/bookcase

кітап сөресі/кітап шкафі

kitap söresi/kitap şkafi

bowl

тостаған

tostağan

cabinet

кабинет

kabïnet

carpet

кілем

kilem

carport

көлік жаппасы

kölik jappası

ceiling

төбе

töbe

cellar

төле

töle

chair

орындық

orındıq

chimney

түтіндік

tütindik

---

clock

сағат

sağat

---

closet

шкаф

şkaf

---

computer

компьютер

komp'yuter

---

couch

диван

dïvan

---

counter

сөре

sore

---

crib

қора

qora

---

cupboard

асадал

asadal

cup

кесе

kese

---

curtain

перде

perde

---

desk

үстел

üstel

---

dining room

ас бөлмесі

as bölmesi

---

dishes

ыдыстар

ıdıstar

---

dishwasher

ыдыс жуғыш машина

ıdıs juğış maşïna

---

door

есік

esik

---

doorbell

есік қоңырауы

esik qoñırauı

---

doorknob

есік тұтқасы

esik tutqası

---

doorway

есік орны

esik ornı

---

drapes

драп

drap

---

drawer

жәшік

jäşik

---

driveway

жол

jol

---

dryer

кептіргіш

keptirgiş

---

duct

құбыр

qubır

---

exterior

сыртқы көрініс

sırtqı körinis

---

family room

ортақ бөлме

ortaq bölme

---

fan

желдеткіш

jeldetkiş

---

faucet

шүмек

şümek

---

fence

дуал

dual

---

fireplace

алауошақ

alauoşaq

---

floor

еден

eden

---

foundation

іргетас

irgetas

---

frame

жақтау

jaqtau

---

freezer

мұздатқыш

muzdatqış

---

furnace

пеш

peş

---

furniture

жиһаз

jïhaz

---

garage

гараж

garaj

---

garden

бақша

baqşa

---

grill

гриль

grïl'

---

gutters

ағынды жыралар

ağındı jıralar

---

hall/hallway

зал/кіреберіс

zal/kireberis

---

hamper

себет

sebet

---

heater

жылытқыш

jılıtqış

---

insulation

оқшаулау

oqşaulau

---

jacuzzi tub

джакузи

djakuzï

---

key

кілт

kilt

---

kitchen

ас бөлмесі

as bölmesi

---

ladder

баспалдақ

baspaldaq

---

lamp

шам

şam

---

landing

жерге қондыру

jerge qondıru

---

laundry

кір жуатын бөлме

kir juatın bölme

---

lawn

көгал алаң

kögal alañ

---

lawnmower

көгал шапқыш

kögal şapqış

---

library

кітапхана

kitapxana

---

light

жарық

jarıq

---

linen closet

көйлек-көншек шкафі

köylek-könşek şkafi

---

living room

қонақ бөлмесі

qonaq bölmesi

---

lock
құлып
qulıp

loft
лофт
loft

mailbox
пошта жәшігі
poşta jäşigi

mantle
мантия
mantïya

master bedroom
үй иелерінің жатын бөлмесі
üy ïeleriniñ jatın bölmesi

microwave
қысқа толқынды пеш
qısqa tolqındı peş

mirror
айна
ayna

neighborhood
көршілес аймақ
körşiles aymaq

nightstand

төсек үстелшесі

tösek üstelşesi

---

office

кеңсе

keñse

---

oven

пеш

peş

---

painting

көркем сурет

körkem suret

---

paneling

панельмен қаптау

panel'men qaptau

---

pantry

қойма

qoyma

---

patio

ішкі аула

işki aula

---

picnic table

пикник үстелі

pïknïk üsteli

picture

сурет

suret

---

picture frame

сурет жиектемесі

suret jïektemesi

---

pillow

жастық

jastıq

---

plates

тарелкелер

tarelkeler

---

plumbing

су құбыры

su qubırı

---

pool

жүзу әуіті

jüzu äuiti

---

porch

кіреберіс

kireberis

---

queen bed

кереует

kereuet

---

quilt

сырылған көрпе

sırılğan körpe

---

railing

таяныш

tayanış

---

range

плита

plïta

---

refrigerator

тоңазытқыш

toñazıtqış

---

remote control

қашықтықтан басқару

qaşıqtıqtan basqaru

---

roof

шатыр

şatır

---

room

бөлме

bölme

---

rug

алаша

alaşa

---

screen door
кіріп-шығатын есік
kirip-şığatın esik

shed
сарай
saray

shelf/shelves
сөре/сөрелер
söre/söreler

shingle
жұмыр тас
jumır tas

shower
душ
duş

shutters
жалюзи
jalyuzï

siding
әрлеу
ärleu

sink
құйылыс
quyılıs

sofa

диван

dïvan

stairs/staircase

баспалдақ

baspaldaq

step

қадам

qadam

stoop

дәліз

däliz

stove

пеш

peş

study

зерттеу

zertteu

table

үстел

üstel

telephone

телефон

telefon

television

теледидар

teledïdar

toaster

тостер

toster

toilet

дәретхана

däretxana

towel

сүлгі

sülgi

trash can

қоқыс шелегі

qoqıs şelegi

trim

қаптау

qaptau

upstairs

жоғарғы қабат

joğarğı qabat

utility room

қосалқы бөлімше

qosalqı bölimşe

vacuum
вакум
vakum

vanity
туалет үстелшесі
tualet üstelşesi

vase
сауыт
sauıt

vent
вентиль
ventïl'

wall
қабырға
qabırğa

wardrobe
көйлек-көншек шкафы
köylek-könşek şkafı

washer/washing machine
кір жуғыш машина
kir juğış maşïna

waste basket
қалдықтар себеті
qaldıqtar sebeti

water heater

су жылытқыш

su jılıtqış

---

welcome mat

қош келдіңіз кілемшесі

qoş keldiñiz kilemşesi

---

window

терезе

tereze

---

window pane

терезе әйнегі

tereze äynegi

---

window sill

терезе алды тақтайы

tereze aldı taqtayı

---

yard

аула

aula

Related Verbs
Қатысты етістіктер

Qatıstı etistikter

to build

құру

quru

---

to buy

сату

satu

to clean

тазарту

tazartu

to decorate

әшекейлеу

äşekeyleu

to leave

кету

ketu

to move in

көшіп келу

köşip kelu

to move out

көшіп кету

köşip ketu

to renovate

жөндеу

jöndeu

to repair

қалпына келтіру

qalpına keltiru

to sell

сату

satu

---

to show

көрсету

körsetu

---

to view

анықтап қарау

anıqtap qarau

---

to visit

кіріп шығу

kirip şığu

---

to work

жұмыс жасау

jumıs jasau

Mike and Linda just bought their first **house**. It is a not a large house, but it is very cozy. It is in a very nice **neighborhood** and has a cute, well-manicured **lawn**. It has a small front **porch**, which will be nice to relax on in the evenings after work. The **exterior** is light blue with a dark blue **door** and **shutters**. It has a nice size **garage** that is big enough for both of their cars and a small **shed** out back for their **lawnmower**. The **backyard** is small, but has a cute little swing set. One day, maybe they will have kids to enjoy it. The **living room** is very spacious and is beautifully decorated in greens and blues. The **walls** are painted light blue and the **curtains** are patterned green and blue. The **couch** and **chair** are very comfortable and roomy enough for the few guests they may have on occasion. Mike is very excited about the new **television** they had installed on the **wall** above the **fireplace**. The **kitchen** is small, yet functional. It has a **refrigerator**, a **dishwasher,** an **oven**, and a built-in **microwave.** There is not much storage, so Linda will have to be very organized. The **walls** are painted yellow and it has a nice floral border. Linda did not pick it out, but it suits her taste well. The **house** has three **bedrooms**, which gives their family room to grow. The **master bedroom** is big enough to fit their **queen bed**, two **nightstands**, and a **dresser**. Linda has already picked out **curtains** to match the bedding. The **walls** are painted beige, but Linda thinks she can brighten the **room** with other decor. Linda's favorite part of the house is the master **bathroom**; it has a jacuzzi **tub** and she can't wait to try it out. It also has a separate **shower** and a double **vanity**. Mike works from home, so he plans to use one of the other, even smaller **bedrooms** as a home **office**. There is not a lot of space, but enough for his **desk, computer**, and a **bookshelf**. The back **porch** is nice and has a charcoal **grill** and a **picnic table.** Mike loves to cook on the **grill**, so it will be put to good use. They will need to get a **washing machine** and **dryer** for the **laundry room,** it is small, but it has a **sink,** which is very helpful when washing clothes. Overall, Mike and Linda picked out an excellent first home. It fits their budget, as well as their taste perfectly!

Майк пен Линда өздерінің бірінші **үйін** жаңа ғана сатып алған кезі еді. Бұл үлкен үй емес, бірақ өте ыңғайлы. Ол өте жақсы **аймақта** орналасқан және ұқыпты, жақсы қиылған **көгалы** бар. Оның алдында жұмыстан шаршап келгенде кешкісін демалуға болатын кішкентай алдыңғы

кіреберісі бар. **Сырты** ақшыл көк, қара көк **есігі** және **терезе қақпақтарымен**. . Екеуінің де көлігі сыятындай өлшемі жақсы **гараж** және артта **көгал шапқыш** қоюға арналған кішкентай **сарай** бар. **Артқы ауласы** кішкентай, бірақ әдемі **әткеншектер** бар. Бір күні мүмкін сол әткеншектерді қызықтайтын олардың балалары болар. **Ортақ бөлме** өте кең және жасыл мен көк түстермен өте әдемі әшекейленген. **Қабырғалар** ашық көк түспен боялған және **перделер** жасыл мен көк түстерді қайталайды. **Диван** мен **орындық** өте ыңғайлы және қонақ шақыратын жағдай үшін жайлы кең. Майк **алауошақтың** үстіне **қабырғаға** орналастырылған жаңа **теледидарға** өте қуанышты. **Ас бөлмесі** кішкентай, бірақ функционалды. Мұнда **тоңазытқыш, ыдыс жуғыш машина, пеш** және ішіне қондырылған **қысқа толқынды пеш** бар. Сақтайтын көп орын болмағандықтан, Линдаға барлығын ойластыруы қажет болады. **Қабырғалар** сары түске боялған және оның жақсы гүлді шекарасы бар. Линда бұны өзі таңдаған жоқ, бірақ ол оның көңілінен шықты. **Үйде үш жатын** бөлме бар, олардың отбасыларының өсуіне мүмкіндік береді. **Үй иелерінің жатын бөлмесінің** кеңдігі **кереуетін, төсек үстелшесі** мен **туалет үстелшесі** сыюына сәйкес келеді. Линда төсек құралдарына сәйкес келетін **перделер** сатып алды. **Жар** ақсары түске боялған. Бірақ Линда **бөлмені** басқа түспен бояуды ойлады. Үйдегі Линданың ең сүйікті жері – негізгі **жуынатын бөлме**. Мұнда **джакузи** бар және ол оған түсіп көруге асығуда. Сонымен қатар, мұнда бөлек **душ** және екі **туалет үстелшелері** бар. Майк үйде жұмыс жасайды, сондықтан ол кіші **жатын бөлмесін кеңсе** ретінде пайдалануды жоспарлайды. Бұнда онша көп орын жоқ, бірақ оның **үстелі, компьютер** және **кітап сөресін**

орналастыруға жеткілікті. Артқы **кіреберіс** жақсы және онда **гриль** және **пикник үстелі** бар. Майк **грильде** ас әзірлегенді ұнатады, сондықтан ол пайдалануға қажет болады. **Кір жуатын бөлмеге** олар кір **жуғыш машина** мен **кептіргішті** алу керек. Бұл кішкентай бөлме, бірақ мұнда **құйылыс** бар, бұл кір жуғанда өте пайдалы. Жалпы Майк пен Линда бірінші үйін жақсы алды. Бұл үй олардың бюджеті мен талғамына әмбебап сәйкес келеді!

Mayk pen Lïnda özderiniñ birinşi **üyin** jaña ğana satıp alğan kezi edi. Bul ülken üy emes, biraq öte ıñğaylı. Ol öte jaqsı **aymaqta** ornalasqan jäne uqıptı, jaqsı qiılğan **kögalı** bar. Onıñ aldında jumıstan şarşap kelgende keşkisin demaluğa bolatın kişkentay aldıñğı **kireberisi** bar. **Sırtı** aqşıl kök, qara kök **esigi** jäne **tereze qaqpaqtarımen**. Ekeuiniñ de köligi sıyatınday ölşemi jaqsı **garaj** jäne artta **kögal şapqış** qoyuğa arnalğan kişkentay **saray** bar. **Artqı aulası** kişkentay, biraq ädemi ätkenşekter bar. Bir küni mümkin sol ätkenşekterdi qızıqtaytın olardıñ balaları bolar. **Ortaq** bölme öte keñ jäne jasıl men kök tüstermen öte ädemi äşekeylengen. **Qabırğalar** aşıq kök tüspen boyalğan jäne **perdeler** jasıl men kök tüsterdi qaytalaydı. **Dïvan** men **orındıq** öte ıñğaylı jäne qonaq şaqıratın jağday üşin jaylı keñ. Mayk **alauoşaqtıñ** üstine qabırğağa ornalastırılğan jaña **teledïdarğa** öte quanıştı. **As bölmesi** kişkentay, biraq funkcïonaldı. Munda **toñazıtqış, ıdıs juğış maşina, peş** jäne işine qondırılğan **qısqa tolqındı peş** bar. Saqtaytın köp orın bolmağandıqtan, Lïndağa barlığın oylastıruı qajet boladı. **Qabırğalar** sarı tüske boyalğan jäne onıñ jaqsı güldi şekarası bar. Lïnda bunı özi tañdağan joq, biraq ol onıñ köñilinen şıqtı. **Üyde üş jatın** bölme bar, olar ortaq bölmeniñ ösuine mümkindik beredi. **Üy ïeleriniñ jatın bölmesiniñ** keñdigi **kereuetin, tösek üstelşesi** men **tualet üstelşesi** sıyuına säykes keledi. Lïnda tösek quraldarına säykes keletin perdeler satıp aldı. **Jar** aqsarı tüske boyalğan. Biraq Lïnda **bölmeni** basqa tüspen boyaudı oyladı. Üydegi Lïndanıñ eñ süyikti jeri – negizgi **juınatın bölme**. Munda **jakuzï** bar jäne ol oğan tüsip köruge asığuda. Sonımen qatar, munda bölek **duş** jäne eki **tualet üstelşeleri** bar. Mayk üyde jumıs jasaydı, sondıqtan ol kişi **jatın bölmesin keñse** retinde paydalanudı josparlaydı. Bunda onşa köp orın joq, biraq onıñ **üsteli**, **komp'yuter** jäne **kitap söresin** ornalastıruğa jetkilikti. Artqı **kireberis** te jaqsı jäne onda **grïl'** jäne **pïknïk üsteli** bar. Mayk **grïl'de** as äzirlegendi unatadı, sondıqtan ol paydalanuğa qajet boladı. **Kir juatın bölmege** olar **kir juğış maşïna** men **keptirgişti** alu kerek. Bul kişkentay bölme, biraq munda **quyılıs** bar, bul kir juğanda öte paydalı. Jalpı Mayk pen Lïnda birinşi üyin jaqsı aldı. Bul üy olardıñ byudjeti men talğamına ämbebap säykes keledi!

9) Arts & Entertainment
9) Өнер & Сауық
9) Öner & Sauıq

3-D

3-Д

3-D

---

action movie

боевик

boevïk

---

actor/actress

актёр/актрисса

aktyor/aktrïssa

---

album

альбом

al'bom

---

alternative

балама

balama

---

amphitheater

амфитеатр

amfiteatr

---

animation

мультипликация

mul'tïplïkacïya

artist

суретші

suretşi

audience

дәрісхана

därisxana

ballerina

балерина

balerïna

ballet

балет

balet

band

топ

top

blues

блюз

blyuz

caption

қолтаңба

qoltañba

carnival

карнавал

karnaval

cast

актёрлер құрамы

aktyorler quramı

choreographer

балетмейстер

baletmeyster

cinema

кино

kïno

classic

классика

klassïka

comedy

комедия

komedïya

commercial

коммерциялық

kommercïyalıq

composer

сазгер

sazger

concert

концерт

koncert

---

conductor

жолсерік

jolserik

---

contemporary

заманауи

zamanawï

---

country

ел

el

---

credits

несиелер

nesïeler

---

dancer

биші

bïşi

---

director

режиссёр

rejïssyor

---

documentary

көркем фильм

körkem fïl'm

---

drama
драма
drama

drummer
дабылшы
dabılşı

duet
дуэт
duét

episode
эпизод
épïzod

event
оқиға
oqïğa

exhibit
көрме
körme

exhibition
көрме
körme

fair
жәрмеңке
järmeñke

fantasy

фэнтэзи

féntézï

feature/feature film

толықметражды/көркем фильм

tolıqmetrajdı/körkem fil'm

film

фильм

fil'm

flick

фильм

fil'm

folk

халық

xalıq

gallery

галерея

galereya

genre

жанр

janr

gig

концерт

koncert

group

топ

top

guitar

гитара

gïtara

guitarist

гитаршы

gïtarşı

hip-hop

хип-хоп

xïp-xop

horror

қорқыныш

qorqınış

inspirational

шабытты

şabıttı

jingle

шылдыр

şıldır

legend

аңыз

añız

lyrics

лирика

lïrïka

---

magician

сиқыршы

sïqırşı

---

microphone

микрофон

mïkrofon

---

motion picture

кинофильм

kïnofïl'm

---

movie director

кинорежиссёр

kïnorejïssyor

---

movie script

кино сценариі

kïno scenarïi

---

museum

мұражай

murajay

---

music

музыка

muzïka

---

musical

мюзикл

muzıkl

---

musician

музыкант

muzıkant

---

mystery

құпия

qupïya

---

new age

жаңа ғасыр

jaña ğasır

---

opera

опера

opera

---

opera house

опера театры

opera teatrı

---

orchestra

оркестр

orkestr

---

painter

суретші

suretşi

---

painting

сурет өнері

suret öneri

---

parade

шеру

şeru

---

performance

қойылым

qoyılım

---

pianist

пианинода ойнаушы

pïanïnoda oynauşı

---

picture

сурет

suret

---

play

ойын

oyın

---

playwright

драматург

dramaturg

---

pop

поп

pop

---

popcorn

попкорн

popkorn

---

producer

продюсер

prodyuser

---

rap

рэп

rép

---

reggae

рэгги

réggï

---

repertoire

репертуар

repertuar

---

rock

рок

rok

---

role

рөл

röl

---

romance

роман

roman

scene

сахна

saxna

science fiction

ғылыми фантастика

ğılımï fantastïka

sculpter

мүсінші

müsinşi

shot

кадр

kadr

show

шоу

şou

show business

шоу кәсібі

şou käsibi

silent film

дыбыссыз фильм

dıbıssız fïl'm

singer

әнші

änşi

sitcom

ситуациялық комедия

sïtuacïyalıq komedïya

---

soloist

жеке орындаушы

jeke orındauşı

---

song

ән

än

---

songwriter

ән авторы

än avtorı

---

stadium

стадион

stadïon

---

stage

сахна

saxna

---

stand-up comedy

стандап комедиясы

standap komedïyası

---

television

теледидар

teledïdar

TV show

топтама

toptama

---

theater

театр

teatr

---

understudy

дублёр

dublyor

---

vocalist

вокалшы

vokalşı

---

violinist

скрипкашы

skrïpkaşı

Related Verbs
Қатысты етістіктер
Qatıstı etistikter

---

to act

әрекет ету

äreket etu

---

to applaud

қол соғу

qol soğu

---

to conduct

өткізу

ötkizu

to dance

билеу

bïleu

to direct

басқару

basqaru

to draw

сурет салу

suret salu

to entertain

көңіл көтеру

köñil köteru

to exhibit

көрсету

körsetu

to host

орналастыру

ornalastıru

to paint

бояу

boyau

to perform

қойылым қою

qoyılım qoyu

---

to play

ойнау

oynau

---

to sculpt

мүсіндеу

müsindeu

---

to show

көрсету

körsetu

Mark Jones is a **legend** in **show business**. His career has been nothing less than amazing. He is an award-winning **actor**, **director**, and **producer** of **film** and **television**. Jones was born in West Central, California. His mother was a teacher and his father was a police officer. He came from humble beginnings and built his career from the bottom up. As a boy, he loved to be the center of attention; he either had a **microphone** in his hand or a **guitar** over his shoulder. He was a very talented **musician** and it seemed he was headed on a path towards becoming a **singer**. He is a talented **songwriter** as well. Few people know that he released his first and only **album** when he was just 16 years old. It was a **pop album**, but It didn't have much success. That didn't stop him from finding his purpose. He also tried **stand-up comedy**. He always drew large crowds, but he knew that wasn't what he was called to do. When he was in his early twenties, he decided to try out for the local community **musical**. He was amazing in his **role** and that is when he made the decision to try acting and he has never looked back! His acting career took off fast. He got his start on a **sitcom** called *Best Friends*. That show was very popular and aired for eight full seasons. It was the beginning of Jones' long and successful and career. He went on to star in several **feature films**, such as *The Dollar, Money Maze*, and *Backyard Boys*, just to name a few. There were a few flops in his career, but that didn't stop him. He has starred in many different **genres** of films; proving his versatility as an **actor**. He has played in **dramas, comedies**, and **documentaries**. He has also won multiple major awards for his acting. As time went on, he decided to try **directing films**. He was amazing as a **director** and won awards for his work with **feature films**, such as *The Child* and *End of All*. But that wasn't enough for Mark; he became a **producer** and to no surprise, was very successful. His **films** have been wildly successful and it makes everyone wonder where he will go next. It is safe to call Mark Jones a mega-**star**. He has not only been successful in every **entertainment** venture he has attempted, he has also been successful with his family. He has been married to his wife for twenty-five years, which is a rarity in show business.

Марк Джонс **шоу кәсібінде аңыз** болып табылады. Оның **мансабы** кереметтен төмен болмады. Ол сыймен марапатталған **актёр, режиссёр** және фильм мен **теледидар продюсері.** Джонс Калифорнияның Орталық Батысында туылған. Оның анасы мұғалім және оның әкесі полиция офицері болған. Ол жұпыны жағдаймен келіп, мансабын басынан бастап құрды. Бала кезінен назар ортасында болғанды ұнататын. Ол қолында **микрофон** немесе иығында **гитара** болатын. Ол өте талантты **музыкант** болды және **әнші** болу жолында тұрғандай көрінетін. Сол сияқты ол талантты **ән авторы**. Ол бірінші және жалғыз **альбомын** 16 жасында шығарғанын аз адам біледі. Бұл **поп альбомы** болатын, алайда ол онша сәтті болған жоқ. Бірақ бұл оның мақсатын іздеуден тайдырмады. Ол сонымен қатар, **стандап комедиясын** да сынап көрді. Ол әрдайым көп халықты жинайтын, бірақ оның негізігі қалауы бұл емес екенін білді. Ол жиырманың басында болғанда, жергілікті **мюзикл** қауымдастығында өзін сынап көрмекші болды. Ол өз **рөлін** тамаша ойнады және осы кезде ол актёр болуға шешім қабылдады және бірде бір кейін шегінген емес. Оның актерлық мансабы тез көтерілді. Ол өзінің бірінші рөлін *Жан Достар* атты **ситуациялық комедиядан** бастады. Бұл шоу өте танымал болды және толық сегіз мезгілі көрсетті. Бұл Джонның ұзақ және сәтті мансабының басы еді. Ол *Доллар, Ақша лабиринті* және *Артқы аула балалары* атты **көркем фильмдердің** басты рөлінде ойнады, бұл тек бірнешеуінің атауы ғана. Оның мансабында бірнеше рет сәтсіздіктер болды, бірақ олар оны тоқтатқан емес. Ол басқа фильм **жанрларында** да басты рөлде ойнап, өзінің **актёр** ретінде жан-жақтылығын дәлелдеді. Ол **драма**, **комедия** және **көркем фильмдерінде** де ойнады. Ол өзінің актёрлік шығармашылығы үшін көптеген басты сыйлармен марапатталды. Уақыт өте келе, ол өзі **фильмдерді түсіріп** көруді шешті. Ол **режиссёр** ретінде тамаша нәтижелер көрсетті және *Бала* мен *Барлығының соңы* атты **көркем фильмдері** үшін көптеген сыйлықтар берілді. Бірақ оның бәрі Марк үшін жеткіліксіз болды. Сонымен ол **продюсер** атанды және оның сәтті болуына ешкімді де таң қалдырмады. Оның **фильмдері** ерекше сәтті болды және адамдар оның енді қай салаға баратынын білгісі келді. Марк Джонсты Мега- **жұлдыз** деуге лайықты еді. Ол тек қалаған **сауық** салаларында ғана емес, сонымен қатар ол өз жанұясында да сәтті болды. Ол өз зайыбымен 25 жыл бойына үйленген болды, бұл шоу кәсібінде сирек жағдай.

Mark Jons **şou käsibinde añız** bolıp tabıladı. Onıñ **mansabı** keremetten tömen bolmadı. Ol sıymen marapattalğan **aktyor**, **rejïssyor** jäne fïl'm men teledïdar **prodyuseri**. Jons Kalïfornïyanıñ Ortsalıq Batısında tuılğan. Onıñ anası muğalim jäne onıñ äkesi polïcïya oficeri bolğan. Ol jupını jağdaymen kelip, mansabın basınan bastap qurdı. Bala kezinen nazar ortasında bolğandı unatatın. Ol qolında **mïkrofon** nemese iiğında **gïtara** bolatın. Ol öte talanttı **muzıkant** boldı jäne **änşi** bolu jolında turğanday körinetin. Sol sïyaqtı ol talanttı **än avtorı**. Ol birinşi jäne jalğız **al'bomın** 16 jasında şığarğanın az adam biledi. Bul **pop al'bomı** bolatın, alayda ol onşa sätti bolğan joq. Biraq bul onıñ maqsatın izdeuden taydırmadı. Ol sonımen qatar, **standap komedïyasın** da sınap kördi. Ol ärdayım köp xalıqtı jïnaytın, biraq onıñ negizigi qalauı bul emes ekenin bildi. Ol jiirmanıñ basında bolğanda, jergilikti **myuzïkl** qauımdastığında özin sınap körmekşi boldı. Ol öz **rölin** tamaşa oynadı jäne osı kezde ol aktyor boluğa şeşim qabıldadı jäne birde bir keyin şegingen emes. Onıñ akterlıq mansabı tez köterildi. Ol öziniñ birinşi rölin Jan Dostar attı **sïtuacïyalıq komedïyadan** bastadı. Bul şou öte tanımal boldı jäne tolıq segiz mezgili körsetti. Bul Djonnıñ uzaq jäne sätti mansabınıñ bası edi. Ol Dollar, Aqşa labïrïnti jäne Artqı aula balaları attı **körkem fïl'mderdiñ** bastı rölinde oynadı, bul tek birneşeuiniñ atauı ğana. Onıñ mansabında birneşe ret sätsizdikter boldı, biraq olar onı toqtatqan emes. Ol basqa fïl'm **janrlarında** da bastı rölde oynap, öziniñ **aktyor** retinde janjaqtılığın däleldedi. Ol **drama**, **komedïya** jäne **körkem fil'mderinde** de oynadı. Ol öziniñ aktyorlik şığarmaşılığı üşin köptegen bastı sıylarmen marapattaldı. Waqıt öte kele, ol özi **fil'mderdi tüsirip** körudi şeşti. Ol **rejïssyor** retinde tamaşa nätïjeler körsetti jäne Bala men Barlığınıñ soñı attı **körkem fil'mderi** üşin köptegen sıylıqtar berildi. Biraq onıñ bäri Mark üşin jetkiliksiz boldı. Sonımen ol **prodyuser** atandı jäne onıñ sätti boluına eşkimdi de tañ qaldırmadı. Onıñ **fil'mderi** erekşe sätti boldı jäne adamdar onıñ endi qay salağa baratının bilgisi keldi. Mark Jonstı Mega- **juldız** deuge layıqtı edi. Ol tek qalağan **sauıq** salalarında ğana emes, sonımen qatar ol öz januyasında da sätti boldı. Ol öz zayıbımen 25 jıl boyına üylengen boldı, bul şou käsibinde sirek jağday.

10) Games and Sports
10) Ойындар және спорт түрлері
10) Oyındar jäne sport türleri

ace

тұз

tuz

---

amateur

әуесқой

äuesqoy

---

archery

садақтан жебе ату

sadaqtan jebe atu

---

arena

алаң

alañ

---

arrow

жебе

jebe

---

athlete

атлет

atlet

---

badminton

бадминтон

badmïnton

---

ball

доп

dop

---

base

база

baza

---

baseball

бейсбол

beysbol

---

basket

себет

sebet

---

basketball

баскетбол

basketbol

---

bat

сақа

saqa

---

bicycle

велосипед

velosïped

---

billiards

биллиярд

bïllïyard

---

bow

кегельдер

kegel'der

---

bowling

боулинг

bowlïng

---

boxing

бокс

boks

---

captain

капитан

kapïtan

---

champion

жеңімпаз

jeñimpaz

---

championship

чемпионат

çempïonat

---

cleats

клемма

klemma

---

club

клуб

klub

---

competition

жарыс

jarıs

---

course

курс

kurs

---

court

корт

kort

---

cricket

крикет

krïket

---

cup

кубок

kubok

---

curling

кёрлинг

kurlïng

---

cycling

велосипед айдау

velosïped aydau

---

darts

дартс

darts

---

defense

қорғану

qorğanu

---

diving

дайвинг

dayvïng

---

dodgeball

ұрдажық

urdajıq

---

driver

ұзын доп таяқ

uzın dop tayaq

---

equestrian

ат сайысы

at sayısı

---

event

оқиға

oqïğa

---

fan

табынушы

tabınuşı

---

fencing

семсерлесу

semserlesu

field

алаң

alañ

figure skating

мәнерлеп сырғанау

mänerlep sırğanau

fishing

балық аулау

balıq aulau

football

футбол

futbol

game

ойын

oyın

gear

спорттық киім

sporttıq kïim

goal

гол

gol

golf
гольф
gol'f

golf club
гольф клуб
gol'f klub

gym
спортзал
sportzal

gymnastics
гимнастика
gïmnastïka

halftime
жарты цикл
jartı cïkl

helmet
дулыға
dulığa

hockey
хоккей
xokkey

horse racing
ат жарыс
at jarıs

hunting

аң аулау

añ aulau

---

ice skating

коньки тебу

kon'kï tebu

---

inning

беріс

beris

---

jockey

жоккей

jokkey

---

judo

дзюдо

dzyudo

---

karate

каратэ

karaté

---

kayaking

каякинг

kayakïng

---

kickball

кикбол

kïkbol

lacrosse

лакросс

lakross

---

league

лига

lïga

---

martial arts

жекпе-жек өнерлері

jekpe-jek önerleri

---

mat

кілемше

kilemşe

---

match

матч

matç

---

medal

медаль

medal'

---

net

тор

tor

---

offense

бұзу

buzu

Olympic Games

Олимпиада Ойындары

Olïmpïada Oyındarı

---

pentathlon

бессайыс

bessayıs

---

pitch

беріс

beris

---

play

ойын

oyın

---

player

ойыншы

oyınşı

---

polo

поло

polo

---

pool

бассейн

basseyn

---

pool cue

кий

kïy

---

professional

кәсіпқой

käsipqoy

---

puck

шайба

şayba

---

quarter

ширек

şirek

---

race

бәйге

bäyge

---

race car

бәйге көлігі

bäyge köligi

---

racket

ракетка

raketka

---

record

есеп беру

esep beru

---

referee

ойын төрешілері

oyın töreşileri

---

relay

реле

rele

---

riding

атпен жүру

atpen jüru

---

ring

шаршы алаңы

şarşı alañı

---

rink

мұз айдыны

muz aydını

---

rowing

ескек

eskek

---

rugby

регби

regbï

---

running

жүгіру

jügiru

---

saddle

ер-тоқым

er-toqım

---

sailing

жүзу

jüzu

score

есеп

esep

shuffleboard

шаффлборд

şafflbord

shuttle cock

волан

volan

skates

коньки

kon'kï

skating

коньки тебу

kon'kï tebu

skiing

шаңғы тебу

şañğı tebu

skis

шаңғы

şañğı

soccer

футбол

futbol

---

softball

софтбол

softbol

---

spectators

көрермендер

körermender

---

sport

спорт

sport

---

sportsmanship

спорт шеберлігі

sport şeberligi

---

squash

сквош

skvoş

---

stadium

стадион

stadïon

---

surf

соқпа толқыны

soqpa tolqını

---

surfboard

сёрфингке арналған тақтай

serfingke arnalğan taqtay

---

swimming

жүзу

jüzu

---

table tennis/ping pong

үстел теннисі

üstel tennïsi

---

tag

белгі

belgi

---

team

топ

top

---

tennis

теннис

tennïs

---

tetherball

тетербол

teterbol

---

throw

лақтыру

laqtıru

track

атлетика

atletïka

---

track and field

жеңіл атлетика

jeñil atletïka

---

volleyball

воллейбол

volleybol

---

water skiing

су шаңғы спорты

su şañğı sportı

---

weight lifting

салмақ көтеру

salmaq köteru

---

whistle

ысқыру

ısqıru

---

win

ұту

utu

---

windsurfing

жел сёрфингі

jel syorfïngi

---

winner

жеңімпаз

jeñimpaz

---

wrestling

күрес

küres

Related Verbs
Қатысты етістіктер

Qatıstı etistikter

---

to catch

қағып алу

qağıp alu

---

to cheat

алдау

aldau

---

to compete

бәсекелесу

bäsekelesu

---

to dribble

тамшылау

tamşılau

---

to go

жүру

jüru

---

to hit

шабуыл жасау

şabuıl jasau

to jump

секіру

sekiru

to kick

тебу

tebu

to knock out

қағып түсіру

qağıp tüsiru

to lose

ұтылу

utılu

to play

ойнау

oynau

to race

жарысу

jarısu

to run

жүгіру

jügiru

to score

есептеу

esepteu

---

to win

жеңу

jeñu

Sports are an important part of our culture and have been throughout all history. Men specifically, are drawn to **sports** because of their competitive nature. From the time they are four or five years old, little boys are playing **sports** such as **baseball, soccer**, and **basketball**. They grow up to be men and their competitive nature grows with them. Contact **sports**, such as American **football, dodgeball, boxing, hockey**, and **wrestling** are popular among men because of their competitiveness. Women also enjoy **sports**, but usually prefer **sports** with less contact, such as **tennis, figure skating, gymnastics**, and **swimming**. In recent years, women are participating in more contact **sports** than ever before. Even retirees enjoy playing **sports, games** such as **golf** and **shuffleboard** are popular among the older crowd. Not only do people enjoy playing **sports**, they love to watch **sports** as well. Wherever you travel, you are sure to see a **fan** or two dressed in their favorite **team** colors. **Sports fan** merchandise is a huge industry. **Sports fans** spend a lot of money every year to buy **tickets** to events to cheer on their **team**. The most popular sporting **event** in the world is the **Olympic Games**. Most **athletes** dream of becoming an **Olympic medalist**. Although, there are some similarities, the **event** has changed quite a bit over the years. The **Olympics** have a rich history and began in

Greece. **Sports** played an important role in Greek culture; playing a part in religious festivals as well as used as training for the Greek military. The **Olympics** began as a festival of **sporting events** that was very popular among the people; there were over 30 thousand **spectators** in attendance. The Greeks competed in **track and field events**, such as **running**, **javelin**, **long jump**, **discus**, just to name a few. The also **wrestled** and had **boxing matches**. The most popular event was the **pentathlon**, which included five **events**: the **long jump**, **javelin**, **discus**, a foot **race**, and **boxing**. The **Olympic Games** and the **sports** involved have changed since that first **event**. Today's **Olympic Games** are held in a different city each year. Over 10 thousand **athletes** compete in over 300 **events**! Some of the sports in the Modern **Olympic Games** are **archery**, **diving**, **basketball**, **cycling**, **volleyball**, **boxing**, and the modern **pentathlon** which includes **fencing**, **swimming**, show jumping**(equestrian)**, pistol **shooting**, and a cross country **run.**

Спорт біздің мәдениетіміздің маңызды бөлігі және тарихтың барлық кезеңінде де болған. Ер адамдар **спортқа** ерекше құмар, өйткені оларда көбіне бәсекелестік мінез қалыптасқан. Уақыт өте келе олар төрт немесе бес жасар болғанда, кішкентай балалар **баскетбол**, **футбол** және **бейсбол** сияқты **спорт** түрлерімен шұғылданады. Олар ер азамат болып өскендіктен, олардың бәсекелестік мінездері де олармен бірге өседі. Американдық **футбол, ұрдажық, бокс, хоккей** және **күрес** сияқты жанасуы көп **спорт** түрлері өздерінің бәсекелестігіне байланысты ер адамдардың арасында ерекше танымал болып табылады. Әйел адамдар да **спортты** ұнатады, алайда олар **теннис, мәнерлеп**

сырғанау, **гимнастика** және **жүзу** сияқты жанасуы аз спорт түрлерін артық көреді. Соңғы жылдарда әйел адамдар бұрыңғымен салыстырғанда, жанасқан **спорт** түрлерімен көбірек шұғылданады. Тіпті қарт адамдар да үлкендердің арасында танымал **гольф** және **шаффлборд** сияқты **спорт** пен **ойын** түрлерін ұнатады. Адамдар тек **спортпен** шұғылдануды ғана емес, сонымен қатар **спортты** бақылағанды да ұнатады. Сіз қайда саяхаттасаңыз да, ұнататын тобының түстерін киіп алған бір немесе екі **табынушыларды** міндетті түрде кездестіресіз. **Спорттық табынушылардың** тауарлары бұл үлкен өндіріс. **Спорттық табынушылар** өз **тобына** болысуға спорттық **оқиғаға** қатысу мақсатында **билет** алу үшін жыл сайын көптеген қаражат жұмсайды. Әлемдегі ең әйгілі **спорт** оқиғасы бұл **Олимпиада Ойындары**. Көптеген **атлеттер Олимпиадалық медаль иегері** болуды армандайды. Ортақ белгілері болғанымен, жылдар бойы көп зат өзгерді. **Олимпиада ойындарының** бай тарихы бар және ол Грециядан басталды. **Спорт** Греция мәдениетінде маңызды рөл атқарды, діни фестивалінің бөлігі ретінде де және сол сияқты Грецияның қарулы күштерін жаттықтыру мақсатында да пайдаланылды. **Олимпиада ойындары** адамдар арасында өте танымал **спорттық оқиғалар** фестивалі ретінде басталды. Мұнда 30 мыңнан астам **көрермендер** болатын. Гректер **жүгіру, найза лақтыру, ұзындыққа секіру, диск лақтыру** сияқты **жеңіл атлетикаға** қатысқан, бұл тек аз ғана атаулары. Сонымен қатар, **күрес** және **бокс жарыстары**. Ең танымал оқиға бұл **бессайыс**, оның ішіне: **ұзындыққа секіру, найза лақтыру, диск лақтыру, аяқ жарысы** және **бокс** кіретін. **Олимпиада Ойындары** және оның ішіне кіретін басқа да **спорт** түрлері сол бірінші спорттық оқиғадан кейін біраз өзгеріске ұшырады. Бүгінгі **Олимпиада Ойындары** жыл сайын әртүрлі қалаларда өткізіледі. 10 мыңнан астам **атлеттер** 300 оқиғада жарысады! Заманауи **Олимпиада Ойындарының** ішіне кіретін кейбір **спорт** түрлері: **садақтан жебе ату, дайвинг, баскетбол, велосипед айдау, воллейбол, бокс** және заманауи **бессайыс**, оның ішіне кіретін: **семсерлесу, жүзу**, секіру шоуы (**ат сайысы**), **тир** және **кросс жүгіру**.

Sport bizdiñ mädenïetimizdiñ mañızdı böligi jäne tarïxtıñ barlıq kezeñinde de bolğan. Er adamdar **sportqa** erekşe qumar, öytkeni olarda köbine bäsekelestik minez qalıptasqan. Waqıt öte kele olar tört nemese bes jasar bolğanda, kişkentay balalar **basketbol**, **futbol** jäne **beysbol** sïyaqtı **sport** türlerimen şuğıldanadı. Olar er azamat bolıp öskendikten, olardıñ bäsekelestik minezderi de olarmen birge ösedi. Amerïkandıq **futbol**, **urdajıq**, **boks**, **xokkey** jäne **küres** sïyaqtı janasuı köp **sport** türleri özderiniñ bäsekelestigine baylanıstı er adamdardıñ arasında erekşe tanımal bolıp tabıladı. Äyel adamdar da **sporttı** unatadı, alayda olar **tennïs**, **mänerlep sırğanau**, **gïmnastïka** jäne **jüzu** sïyaqtı janasuı az sport türlerin artıq köredi. Soñğı jıldarda äyel adamdar burıñğımen salıstırğanda, janasqan sport türlerimen köbirek şuğıldanadı. Tipti qart adamdar da ülkenderdiñ arasında tanımal gol'f jäne **şafflbord** sïyaqtı **sport** pen **oyın** türlerin unatadı. Adamdar tek **sportpen** şuğıldanudı ğana emes, sonımen qatar **sporttı** baqılağandı da unatadı. Siz qayda sayaxattasañız da, unatatın tobınıñ tüsterin kïip alğan bir nemese eki **tabınuşılardı** mindetti türde kezdestiresiz. Sporttıq tabınuşılardıñ tauarları bul ülken öndiris. **Sporttıq tabınuşılar** öz **tobına** bolısuğa sporttıq **oqïğağa** qatısu maqsatında **bïlet** alu üşin jıl sayın köptegen qarajat jumsaydı. Älemdegi eñ äygili **sport** oqïğası bul **Olïmpïada Oyındarı**. Köptegen **atletter Olïmpïadalıq medal' ïegeri** boludı armandaydı. Ortaq belgileri bolğanımen, jıldar boyı köp zat özgerdi. **Olïmpïada oyındarynıñ** bay tarïxı bar jäne ol Grecïyadan bastaldı. **Sport** Grecïya mädenïetinde mañızdı röl atqardı, dinï festïvaliniñ böligi retinde de jäne sol sïyaqtı Grecïyanıñ qarulı küşterin jattıqtıru maqsatında da paydalanıldı. **Olïmpïada Oyındary** adamdar arasında öte tanımal **sporttıq oqïğalar** festïvali retinde bastaldı. Munda 30 mıñnan astam **körermender** bolatın. Grekter **jügiru, nayza laqtıru, uzındıqqa sekiru, dïsk laqtıru** sïyaqtı **jeñil atletïkağa** qatısqan, bul tek az ğana atauları. Sonımen qatar, **küres** jäne **boks jarıstarı**. Eñ tanımal oqïğa bul **bessayıs**, onıñ işine: **uzındıqqa sekiru, nayza laqtıru, dïsk laqtıru, ayaq jarısı** jäne **boks** kiretin. **Olïmpïada Oyındary** jäne onıñ işine kiretin basqa da **sport** türleri sol birinşi **sporttıq oqïğadan** keyin biraz özgeriske uşıradı. Bügingi **Olïmpïada Oyındary** jıl sayın ärtürli qalalarda ötkiziledi. 10 mıñnan astam **atletter** 300 oqïğada jarısadı! Zamanauï **Olïmpïada Oyındarynıñ** işine kiretin keybir **sport** türleri: **sadaqtan jebe atu, dayvïng, basketbol, velosïped aydau, volleybol, boks** jäne zamanauï **bessayıs**, onıñ işine kiretin: **semserlesu, jüzu,** sekiru şouı (**at sayısı), tïr** jäne **kross jügiru**.

11) Food
11) Ac
11) As

apple

алма

alma

---

bacon

бекон

bekon

---

bagel

тоқаш

toqaş

---

banana

банан

banan

---

beans

атбасбұршақ

atbasburşaq

---

beef

сиыр еті

sïr eti

---

bread

нан

nan

broccoli

брокколи

brokkolï

brownie

брауни

brawnï

cake

торт/бәліш

tort/bäliş

candy

кәмпит

kämpït

carrot

сәбіз

säbiz

celery

балдыркөк

baldırkök

cheese

ірімшік

irimşik

cheesecake
ірімшік бәліші
irimşik bälişi

---

chicken
тауық еті
tauıq eti

---

chocolate
шоколад
şokolad

---

cinnamon
даршын
darşın

---

cookie
печенье
peçen'e

---

crackers
крекерлер
krekerler

---

dip
тұздық
tuzdıq

---

eggplant
баялды
bayaldı

---

fig
інжір
injir

fish
балық
balıq

fruit
жеміс
jemis

garlic
сарымсақ
sarımsaq

ginger
жанжабіл
janjabil

ham
ветчина
vetçïna

herbs
шөптер
şöpter

honey
бал
bal

ice cream

балмұздақ

balmuzdaq

---

jelly/jam

джем

jem

---

ketchup

кетчуп

ketçup

---

lemon

лимон

lïmon

---

lettuce

салат

salat

---

mahi mahi

мөңке балық

mönke balıq

---

mango

манго

mango

---

mayonnaise

майонез

mayonez

---

meat

ет

et

---

melon

қауын

qauın

---

milk

сүт

süt

---

mustard

қыша

qışa

---

noodles

кеспе

kespe

---

nuts

жаңғақтар

jañğaqtar

---

oats

сұлы

sulı

---

olive

зәйтүн

zäytün

---

orange
апельсин
apel'sïn

pasta
макарондық өнімдер
makarondıq önimder

pastry
кондитерлік өнімдер
kondïterlik önimder

pepper
бұрыш
burış

pork
шошқа еті
şoşqa eti

potato
картоп
kartop

pumpkin
асқабақ
asqabaq

raisin
мейіз
meyiz

sage

жалб**ы**з

jalbız

salad

салат

salat

salmon

албырт

albırt

sandwich

сэндвич

séndvïç

sausage

шұж**ы**қ

şujıq

soup

сорпа

sorpa

squash

асқабақ

asqabaq

steak

стейк

steyk

strawberry

құлпынай

büldirgen

sugar

қант

qant

tea

шай

şay

toast

тост

tost

tomato

қызанақ

qızanaq

vinegar

сірке суы

sirke suı

vegetables

көкөністер

kökönister

water

су

su

wheat

бидай

bïday

Restaurants and Cafes
Мейрамханалар мен Дәмханалар
Meyramxanalar men Dämxanalar

---

a la carte

тапсырысқа

tapsırısqa

---

a la mode

сәнді

sändi

---

appetizer

жеңіл тамақ

jeñil tamaq

---

bar

бар

bar

---

beverage

сусын

susın

---

bill

шот

şot

---

bistro

бистро

bïstro

---

boiled bowl

қайнатылған тостаған

qaynatılğan tostağan

---

braised

сөндірілген

söndirilgen

---

breakfast

таңғы ас

tañğı as

---

brunch

кеш таңғы асы

keş tañğı asɪ

---

cafe/cafeteria

дәмхана

dämxana

---

cashier

кассир

kassïr

---

chair

үстел

üstel

---

charge

төлем

tölem

---

check

чек

çek

---

chef

аспазшы

aspazşı

---

coffee

кофе

kofe

---

coffee shop

кофехана

kofexana

---

condiments

дәмдеуіштер

dämdeuişter

---

cook

ас әзірлеу

as äzirleu

---

courses

курстар

kurstar

---

credit card

кредиттік карта

kredïttik karta

---

cup

кесе

kese

---

cutlery

ас құралдары

as quraldarı

---

deli/delicatessen

жеңсік ас

jeñsik as

---

dessert

десерт

desert

---

dine

кешкі ас ішу

keşki as işu

---

diner

келуші

keluşi

---

dinner

кешкі ас

keşki as

---

dish

ыдыс-аяқ

ıdıs-ayaq

dishwasher

ыдыс жуғыш

ıdıs juğış

doggie bag

қалған асқа арналған қап

qalğan asqa arnalğan qap

drink

сусын

susın

entree

кіретін есік

kiretin esik

food

тамақ

tamaq

fork

шанышқы

şanışqı

glass

стакан

stakan

gourmet

тамақ талғағыш

tamaq talğağış

---

hor d'oeuvre

қосымша тағам

qosımşa tağam

---

host/hostess

қожайын

qojayın

---

knife

пышақ

pışaq

---

lunch

түскі ас

tüski as

---

maitre d'

бас даяшы

bas dayaşı

---

manager

басқарушы

basqaruşı

---

menu

ас мәзірі

as mäziri

---

mug

саптыаяқ

saptıayaq

napkin

майлық

maylıq

order

тапсырыс

tapsırıs

party

жиын той

jïın toy

plate

тәрелке

tärelke

platter

тағам

tağam

reservation

орын сақтау

orın saqtau

restaurant

мейрамхана

meyramxana

saucer

табақша

tabaqşa

---

server

қызметші

qızmetşi

---

side order

гарнир

garnïr

---

silverware

күміс ас құралдары

kümis as quraldarı

---

special

арнайы

arnayı

---

spoon

қасық

qasıq

---

starters

бастапқы ас

bastapqı as

---

supper

кешкі ас

keşki as

---

table

үстел

üstel

---

tax

салық

salıq

---

tip

шайпұл

şaypul

---

to go

өзімен бірге

özimen birge

---

utensils

ыдыс

ıdıs

---

waiter/waitress

даяшы

dayaşı

Related Verbs

Қатысты етістіктер

Qatıstı etistikter

to bake

пісіру

pisiru

---

to be hungry

аш болу

aş bolu

to cook

ас әзірлеу

as äzirleu

to cut

кесу

kesu

to drink

ішу

işu

to eat

жеу

jeu

to eat out

ас ішуге бару

as işuge baru

to feed

тамақтандыру

tamaqtandıru

to grow

өсу

ösu

to have breakfast

таңғы ас ішу

tañğı as işu

---

to have lunch

түскі ас ішу

tüski as işu

---

to have dinner

түскі ас ішу

tüski as işu

---

to make

жасау

jasau

---

to order

тапсырыс беру

tapsırıs beru

---

to pay

төлеу

töleu

---

to prepare

дайындау

dayındau

---

to request

сұрау

surau

---

to reserve

орын сақтау

orın saqtau

---

to serve

қызмет ету

qızmet etu

---

to set the table

үстелді тамақ ішуге даярлау

üsteldi tamaq işuge dayarlau

---

to taste

дәмін көру

dämin köru

John and Mary have been dating for quite some time now. Next week is their two year anniversary and John wants to make it really special. Mary really enjoys a nice **steak dinner** out, so John is going to make **reservations** at her favorite **restaurant**. She will be so surprised because they haven't eaten there in a while and she just loves their **salad** and **bread**. John calls and speaks to the **manager** ahead of time to set up the **reservation**. Finally, the day arrives and John picks Mary up at her home. She still doesn't know where they are going, but is excited for the surprise. "Where are we going? Mary asked. "I told you, it's a surprise!" said John. So Mary begins trying to guess where their surprise destination is. "Is it our favorite **diner**? I love the laid back atmosphere and the **waitress** is so nice." "Is it the **coffee shop** on the corner? You know how much I love **coffee**." They arrive at the **restaurant** and she squeals with delight at the thought of the **cheesecake** that they serve for **dessert** . The **host** greets them at the door and promptly seats them at their favorite **table** near the **bar**. It is a quiet little corner of the **restaurant**. The server greets them, lays a **napkin** and **silverware** on their **table**, and then takes their **drink order**. She offers them an **appetizer** while they wait. When the **server** returns, she begins to tell the couple about the daily **specials**. "We'll have two of your best steak **dinners**." John said, "Nothing but the best for my girl!" They are really enjoying their **gourmet meal** and the conversation is great, as always. I think we should have **dessert** for this special night. John tells the **server** that they would like a **brownie a la mode t**o share. The server brings the delicious brownie on a **plate** with two **spoons**. John and Mary both look at the **dessert** and decide they do not have room to eat it. "I think we will need that **to-go**," said Mary. While waiting for the server to pack up their **doggie bag**, John surprised Mary by getting down on his knee to propose! The whole **restaurant** was clapping; even the **dishwasher** and **cooks** came out to congratulate the couple. What a wonderful second anniversary this turned out to be for the happy couple. Now, every year on their anniversary, they **dine** at their favorite **restaurant** to celebrate such a wonderful evening.

Джон мен Мэридің кездесіп жүргендеріне біраз уақыт болды. Келесі аптада олардың екі жылдық мерекесі және Джон оны ерекше қылып өткізгісі келеді. Мэри **кешкі асқа стейк** жеуге барғанды ұнатады, сондықтан Джон оның сүйікті **мейрамханасында орындар сақтап** қоймақшы. Ол қатты таң қалатын болады, өйткені ол жерге көптен бармаған еді және ол ондағы **салат** пен **нанын** ұнататын. Джон ертерек **орындарды сақтап қою** үшін телефон соғып, **менеджермен** сөйлесіп қойды. Нәтижесінде күн жақындағанда Джон Мэриді үйінен алып кетеді. Мэри әлі де олардың қайда баратынын білмейді, бірақ тосын сыйға қуанды. "Біздер қайда барамыз?" деп сұрады Мэри."Мен саған айттым ғой, бұл тосын сый!" деді Джон. Сөйтіп Мэри тосын сыйдың бағытын болжай бастады. "Ол біздің сүйікті **дәмханамыз** ба? Маған ондағы тыныш атмосферасы және **даяшысы** ұнайды." "Бұрыштағы **кофехана** ма? Менің **кофені** қалай сүйетінімді сен жақсы білесің." Олар **мейрамхананың** қасына келеді және ол мұнда **десертке ірімшік бәлішін** беретіндігі есіне түсіп, қатты қуанады. **Бас даяшы** оларды есіктің алдынан күтіп алып, **бардың** қасындағы олардың сүйікті **үстеліне** отырғызады. Бұл **мейрамхананың** жайлы кішкентай бұрышы. Қызметші сәлемдесіп, олардың үстеліне **майлықтар** мен **күміс ас құралдарын** қояды, және кейін олардың **сусын тапсырысын** алады. Ол олар күткенше **жеңіл ас** алуын ұсынды. **Қызметші** қайтып келген соң, ол бүгінгі **арнайы** дайындалған тағамдарды айта бастады."Бізде сіздердің екі ең жақсы **стейк түскі асымыз** болады." "Менің қызыма тек ең жақсысы!" деді Джон. Олар ас **талғағыш тағамдарымен** шынайы сүйсінді және әдеттегідей әңгімелері де тамаша болды. Бұл арнайы кеште **дессерт** болуы керек деп ойлаймын. Джон қызметшіге **сәнді брауни** қалайтынын айтты. **Қызметші** ғажайып брауниді **тәрелкеге** салып, екі **шанышқымен** алып келді. Джон және Мэри **дессертке** қарады да, оны жеуге орын жоқ деп шешті. "Мен бұны өзімізбен бірге алу керек деп ойлаймын, "деді Мэри. Олар қызметшінің **қалған асты қапқа** салғанын күтіп отырғанда, Джон бір тізерлеп, оған тұрмысқа шығуын сұрап, Мэриді таң қалдырды. Барлық **мейрамхана** қол соқты. Тіпті **ыдыс**

жуғыш пен **аспазшылар** да жұпты құттықтауға шықты. Бұл бақытты жұп үшін қандай екі жылдық мереке болды. Ендігі, жыл сайын олар әрбір жылдық мерекесінде сондай тамаша кешті атап өту үшін өздерінің сүйікті **мейрамханасына кешкі асқа** келеді.

Jon men Mérïdiñ kezdesip jürgenderine biraz waqıt boldı. Kelesi aptada olardıñ eki jıldıq merekesi jäne Jon onı erekşe qılıp ötkizgisi keledi. Mérï **keşki asqa steyk** jeuge barğandı unatadı, sondıqtan Jon onıñ süyikti **meyramxanasında orındar saqtap** qoymaqşı. Ol qattı tañ qalatın boladı, öytkeni ol jerge köpten barmağan edi jäne ol ondağı **salat** pen **nanın** unatatın. Jon erterek **orındardı saqtap qoyu** üşin telefon soğıp, **menedjermen** söylesip qoydı. Nätijesinde kün jaqındağanda Jon Mérïdi üyinen alıp ketedi. Mérï äli de olardıñ qayda baratının bilmeydi, biraq tosın cıyğa quandy. "Bizder qayda baramız?" dep suradı Mérï."Men sağan ayttım ğoy, bul tosın sıy!" dedi Jon. Söytip Mérï tosın sıydıñ bağıtın boljay bastadı. "Ol bizdiñ süyikti **dämxanamız** ba? Mağan ondağı tınış atmosferası jäne **dayaşısı** unaydı." "Burıştağı **kofexana** ma? Meniñ **kofeni** qalay süyetinimdi sen jaqsı bilesiñ." Olar **meyramxananıñ** qasına keledi jäne ol munda **desertke irimşik bälişin** beretindigi esine tüsip, qattı quanadı. **Bas dayaşı** olardı esiktiñ aldınan kütip alıp, bardıñ qasındağı olardıñ süyikti **üsteline** otırğızadı. Bul **meyramxananıñ** jaylı kişkentay burışı. Qızmetşi sälemdesip, olardıñ üsteline **maylıqtar** men **kümis as quraldarın** qoyadı, jäne keyin olardıñ **susın tapsırısın** aladı. Ol olar kütkenşe **jeñil as** aluın usındı. **Qızmetşi** qaytıp kelgen soñ, ol bügingi **arnayı** dayındalğan tağamdardı ayta bastadı."Bizde sizderdiñ eki eñ jaqsı **steyk tüski asımız** boladı." "Meniñ qızıma tek eñ jaqsısı!" dedi Jon. Olar as **talğağış tağamdarımen** şınayı süysindi jäne ädettegidey añgimeleri de tamaşa boldı. Bul arnayı keşte **dessert** boluı kerek dep oylaymın. Jon qızmetşige **sändi brawnï** qalaytının ayttı. **Qızmetşi** ğajayıp brawnïdi **tärelkege** salıp, eki **şanışqımen** alıp keldi. Jon jäne Merï **dessertke** qaradı da, onı jeuge orın joq dep şeşti. "Men bunı özimizben birge alu kerek dep oylaymın, "dedi Merï. Olar qızmetşiniñ **qalğan astı qapqa** salğanın kütip otırğanda, Jon bir tizerlep, oğan turmısqa şığuın surap, Merïdi tañ qaldırdı. Barlıq **meyramxana** qol soqtı. Tipti **ıdıs juğış** pen **aspazşılar** da juptı quttıqtauğa şıqtı. Bul baqıttı jup üşin qanday eki jıldıq mereke boldı. Endigi, jıl sayın olar ärbir jıldıq merekesinde sonday tamaşa keşti atap ötu üşin özderiniñ süyikti **meyramxanasına keşki asqa** keledi.

12) Shopping
12) Сауда-Саттық
12) Sauda-Sattıq

bags
сөмке
sömke

---

bakery
наубайхана
naubayxana

---

barcode
код-штрих
kod-ştrïx

---

basket
себет
sebet

---

bookstore
кітап дүкені
kitap dükeni

---

boutique
бутик
butïk

---

browse

қарау

qarau

buggy/shopping cart

бесік арба/дүкен арбашасы

besik arba/düken arbaşası

butcher

қасапшы

qasapşı

buy

сатып алу

satıp alu

cash

қолма-қол ақша

qolma-qol aqşa

cashier

кассир

kassïr

change

киімін ауыстыру

kïimin auıstıru

changing room

киіп көру бөлмесі

kïip köru bölmesi

cheap

арзан

arzan

check

тексеру

tekseru

clearance

тазалау

tazalau

coin

тиын

tïın

convenience store

шағын дүкен

şağın düken

counter

сатушы сөресі

satuşı söresi

credit card

несие картасы

nesïe kartası

customers

сатып алушылар

satıp aluşılar

debit card

дебеттік карта

debettik karta

---

delivery

жеткізу

jetkizu

---

department store

әмбебап дүкені

ämbebap dükeni

---

discount

жеңілдік

jeñildik

---

discount store

жеңілдіктер дүкені

jeñildikter dükeni

---

drugstore/pharmacy

дәріхана

därixana

---

electronic store

электрондық дүкен

élektrondıq düken

---

escalator

эскалатор

éskalator

---

expensive

қымбат

qımbat

flea market

жайма базары

jayma bazarı

florist

флорист

florïst

grocery store

азық-түлік дүкені

azıq-tülik dükeni

hardware

шаруашылық бөлім

şaruaşılıq bölim

jeweler

зергер

zerger

mall

сауда орталығы

sauda ortalığı

market

базар

bazar

meat department

ет бөлімшесі

et bölimşesi

---

music store

музыкалық дүкен

muzıkalıq düken

---

offer

ұсыныс

usınıs

---

pet store

жануарлар дүкені

januarlar dükeni

---

purchase

сатып алу

satıp alu

---

purse

әмиян

ämïyan

---

rack

тіреу

tireu

---

receipt

түбіртек

tübirtek

---

return

қайтару

qaytaru

---

sale

сату

satu

---

sales person

сатушы

satuşı

---

scale

өлшем

ölşem

---

size

өлшем

ölşem

---

shelf/shelves

сөре/сөрелер

söre/söreler

---

shoe store

аяқ киім дүкені

ayaq kïim dükeni

---

shop

дүкен

düken

---

shopping center

сауда орталығы

sauda ortalığı

---

store

дүкен

düken

---

supermarket

әмбебап дүкен

ämbebap düken

---

tailor

тігінші

tiginşi

---

till

касса

kassa

---

toy store

ойыншық дүкені

oyınşıq dükeni

---

wallet

әмиян

ämïyan

---

wholesale

көтерме сауда

köterme sauda

Related Verbs
Қатысты етістіктер
Qatıstı etistikter

to buy

сатып алу

satıp alu

---

to charge

төлеу

töleu

---

to choose

таңдау

tañdau

---

to exchange

алмастыру

almastıru

---

to go shopping

сауда жасауға бару

sauda jasauğa baru

---

to owe

қарыз болу

qarız bolu

---

to pay

төлеу

töleu

---

to prefer

артық көру

artıq köru

---

to return

қайтару

qaytaru

---

to save

сақтау

saqtau

---

to sell

сату

satu

---

to shop

сауда жасау

sauda jasau

---

to spend

жұмсау

jumsau

---

to try on

киіп көру

kiip köru

---

to want

қалау

qalau

It was just a few weeks until Christmas and Mark needed to **purchase** a gift for his wife. He didn't know what he was going to get for her. First, he went to the **bookstore**, she loved to read books. He checked the **shelves** to see if he could find something she had not read before, but he had no luck with that. Then he decided to visit her favorite clothing **boutique**. The **salesperson** was very friendly and helpful as he shopped. She knew his wife and was able to help him with **sizes**. He **browsed** the **racks** for just the right gift, but he did not find anything he thought she would like. Besides, everything was so **expensive**! Next, he went to the **shoe store**. He looked around and just couldn't decide what to get for her, so he left that **store**. He resisted going to the **hardware store**, that is his favorite. He thought to himself, "I have to remember, I am **shopping** for my wife, not me!" He finally decided to go to the **mall**. There are plenty of **shops** there! As he walked through the **mall**, he was getting discouraged; he passed a couple of **department stores**, a **music store** and a **toy store**, but nothing seemed right. Finally, he came upon a **jeweler**. His wife loves jewelry. He approached the **counter** and began telling the **salesman** about his wife and the type of jewelry she wears. He was so excited to learn that the ring he picked out was on **sale**. The **salesman** told him the total and Mark reached for his **wallet** to get the **cash**. He asked the salesman, "Does that **price** include **tax**?" "Yes, of course", replied the **salesman**. Mark realized he didn't have enough **cash**, so he paid with his **credit card**. The salesman thanked him and gave him the ring and **receipt**. Mark was so pleased to have found a gift for his wife. He stopped by the **florist** on the way home to surprise her with some flowers. As he was leaving the **florist**, his wife called and asked him to stop by the **grocery store** on his way home. Mark decided he could get what he needed from the **convenience store**, so he stopped there, and then headed home to his wife. She was so surprised that he bought her flowers. She had a little surprise for him as well; she had stopped at the **bakery** on her way home from work. He thanked her for her thoughtful surprise. How lucky he felt to be in such a giving marriage!

Рождествоға бірнеше ғана апта қалды және Марк зайыбына сыйлық **сатып алуы** тиіс еді. Ол оған не алатынын білмеді. Бірінші, ол **кітап дүкеніне** барды, себебі ол кітап оқығанды ұнатады. Ол оның бұрын оқымаған кітабын табу үшін **сөрелерді** тексерді, бірақ бұл ойы сәтті болмады. Содан ол оның сүйікті киім **бутигіне** баруды шешті. Ол сауда жасау барысында **сатушы** өте жылы шырайлы және көмектесуге дайын болды. Ол оның зайыбын білгендіктен, оған оның өлшемімен көмектесе алды. Ол дұрыс сыйлық таңдау үшін **тіреулерді қарап** шықты, бірақ ол ұнататындай ештеңе таба алмады. Оған қоса, барлығы сондай **қымбат** болды! Келесі ол **аяқ киім дүкеніне** барды. Ол айналасына қарап, оған не алу керектігін шеше алмады, сөйтіп ол дүкеннен шығып кетті. Ол өзі ұнататын **шаруашылық бөлімге** кіруге қарсыласты. Ол ішінен ойлады, "Мен өзіме емес, зайыбыма зат алу үшін **сауда жасауым** керек!" Нәтижесінде ол **сауда орталығына** баруды шешті. Мұнда көптеген **дүкендер** бар. Ол **дүкендердің** арасында жүргенде, сондай абыржыды. Ол біраз дүкендерді: **әмбебап дүкендерін, музыкалық дүкен** және **ойыншық дүкенін** аралап өтті. Бірақ біреуі де дұрыс таңдау болмады. Нәтижесінде, ол **зергерге** келді. Оның зайыбы **зергерлік бұйымдарды** ұнатады. Ол **сатушы сөресіне** жақындады да, сатушыға өзінің зайыбы және оның ұнататын зерлерлік бұйымдары туралы айта бастады. Ол таңдаған сақина **сатылымда** бар екендігін білер кезде сондай қобалжыды. **Сатушы** оның толық бағасын айтты және Марк **қолма-қол ақшамен** төлеу үшін **әмиянын** алды. "Бұл **бағаның** ішіне **салық** кіреді ме?" "Иә, әрине," деп жауап берді **сатушы**. Марк **қолма-қол ақшасының** жетпейтініне көзі жеткен соң, ол **несие картасымен** төледі. Сатушы рахмет айтып, оған сақина мен **түбіртекті** берді. Марк зайыбына сыйлық іздеп тапқанына сондай қуанды. Ол зайыбын бірнеше гүлдермен таң қалдыру үшін үй жолындағы **флористке** жолықты. Ол **флористтен** шығып бара жатқанда, оның зайыбы оған қоңырау шалып, үйге келетін жолдағы **азық-түлік дүкеніне** соғуын сұрады. Марк керек заттың бәрін **шағын дүкеннен** алуды шешіп, сонда жолығып, кейін өз зайыбына үйге бетттеді. Ол оған гүл алғанына сондай қуанды. Оның да оған тосын сыйы бар болып шықты. Ол жұмыстан үйге келе жатқан жолда **наубайханаға** соққан. Ол зайыбын ойлы тосын сыйы үшін алғыс айтты. Ол осындай жанұяда өзін сондай бақытты сезінді!

Rojdestvoğa birneşe ğana apta qaldı jäne Mark zayıbına sıylıq **satıp aluı** tiis edi. Ol oğan ne alatının bilmedi. Birinşi, ol **kitap dükenine** bardı, sebebi ol kitap oqığandı unatadı. Ol onıñ burın oqımağan kitabın tabu üşin **sörelerdi** tekserdi, biraq bul oyı sätti bolmadı. Sodan ol onıñ süyikti kiim **butïgine** barudı şeşti. Ol sauda jasau barısında **satuşı** öte jılı şıraylı jäne kömektesuge dayın boldı. Ol onıñ zayıbın bilgendikten, oğan onıñ ölşemimen kömektese aldı. Ol durıs sıylıq tañdau üşin **tireulerdi qarap** şıqtı, biraq ol unatatınday eşteñe taba almadı. Oğan qosa, barlığı sonday **qımbat** boldı! Kelesi ol **ayaq kiim dükenine** bardı. Ol aynalasına qarap, oğan ne alu kerektigin şeşe almadı, söytip ol dükennen şığıp ketti. Ol özi unatatın **şaruaşılıq bölimge** kiruge qarsılastı. Ol işinen oyladı, "Men özime emes, zayıbıma zat alu üşin **sauda jasauım** kerek!" Nätijesinde ol **sauda ortalığına** barudı şeşti. Munda köptegen **dükender** bar. Ol **dükenderdiñ** arasında jürgende, sonday abırjıdı. Ol birtalay dükenderdi: **ämbebap dükenderin, muzıkalıq düken** jäne **oynşıq dükenin** aralap ötti. Biraq bireui de durıs tañdau bolmadı. Nätijesinde, ol **zergerge** keldi. Onıñ zayıbı **zergerlik buyımdardı** unatadı. Ol **satuşı söresine** jaqındadı da, satuşığa öziniñ zayıbı jäne onıñ unatatın zerlerlik buyımdarı turalı ayta bastadı. Ol tañdağan saqïna **satılımda** bar ekendigin biler kezde sonday qobaljıdı. **Satuşı** onıñ tolıq bağasın ayttı jäne Mark **qolma-qol aqşamen** töleu üşin **ämïyanın** aldı. "Bul **bağanıñ** işine **salıq** kiredi me?" "Ïä, ärïne," dep jauap berdi **satuşı**. Mark qolma-qol aqşasınıñ jetpeytinine közi jetken soñ, ol nesïe kartasımen töledi. Satuşı raxmet aytıp, oğan saqïna men **tübirtekti** berdi. Mark zayıbına sıylıq izdep tapqanına sonday quandı. Ol zayıbın birneşe güldermen tañ qaldıru üşin üy jolındağı **florïstke** jolıqtı. Ol **florïstten** şığıp bara jatqanda, onıñ zayıbı oğan qoñırau şalıp, üyge keletin joldağı **azıq-tülik dükenine** soğuın suradı. Mark kerek zattıñ bärin **şağın dükennen** aludı şeşip, sonda jolığıp, keyin öz zayıbına üyge betttedi. Ol oğan gül alğanına sonday quandı. Onıñ da oğan tosın sıyı bar bolıp şıqtı. Ol jumıstan üyge kele jatqan jolda **naubayxanağa** soqqan. Ol zayıbın oylı tosın sıyı üşin alğıs ayttı. Ol osınday januyada özin sonday baqıttı sezindi!

13) At the Bank
13) Банкте
13) Bankte

account

шот

şot

APR/Annual Percentage Rate

Сәуір/Жылдық Пайыздық Мөлшерлеме

Säuir/Jıldıq Payızdıq Mölşerleme

ATM/Automatic Teller Machine

Банкомат/Банктік автомат

Bankomat/Banktik avtomat

---

balance

теңгерім

teñgerim

---

bank

банк

bank

---

bank charges

банк алымдары

bank alımdarı

---

bank draft

банктік тратта

banktik tratta

---

bank rate

банкінің есеп мөлшерлемесі

bankiniñ esep mölşerlemesi

---

bank statement

банктік үзінді көшірме

banktik üzindi köşirme

---

borrower

қарызгер

qarızger

---

bounced check

қайтарылған чек

qaytarılğan çek

---

cardholder

карточка иеленушісі

kartoçka ïelenuşisi

---

cash

қолма-қол ақша

qolma-qol aqşa

---

cashback

қолма-қол ақшаны қайтару

qolma-qol aqşanı qaytaru

check

тексеру

tekseru

---

checkbook

чек кітапшасы

çek kitapşası

---

checking account

ағымдағы шот

ağımdağı şot

---

collateral

мүлік кепілі

mülik kepili

---

commission

комиссия

komïssïya

---

credit

несие

nesïe

---

credit card

несие картасы

nesïe kartası

---

credit limit

несие лимиті

nesïe lïmïti

---

credit rating

несиелік рейтинг

nesïelik reytïng

---

currency

валюта

valyuta

---

debt

қарыз

qariz

---

debit

дебет

debet

---

debit card

дебет картасы

debet kartası

---

deposit

депозит

depozït

---

direct debit

тікелей дебет

tikeley debet

---

direct deposit

тікелей депозит

tikeley depozït

---

expense

шығыс

şığıs

fees

алымдар

alımdar

foreign exchange rate

айырбас бағамы

ayırbas bağamı

insurance

сақтандыру

saqtandıru

interest

пайыз мөлшері

payız mölşeri

Internet banking

ғаламторлық банктік қызмет көрсету

ğalamtorlıq banktik qızmet körsetu

loan

қарыз

qarız

money

ақша

aqşa

money market

ақша нарығы

aqşa narığı

mortgage

ипотека

ïpoteka

NSF/Insufficient Funds

жеткіліксіз өтеу

jetkiliksiz öteu

online banking

қашықтықтан банктік қызмет көрсету

qaşıqtıqtan banktik qızmet körsetu

overdraft

овердрафт

overdraft

payee

төлемді алушы

tölemdi aluşı

pin number

пин код

pïn kod

register

тіркелу

tirkelu

savings account

жинақ шот

jïnaq şot

statement

үзінді көшірме

üzindi köşirme

tax

салық

salıq

telebanking

телебанкинг

telebankïng

teller

кассир

kassïr

transaction

мәміле

mämile

traveler's check

саяхатшы чегі

sayaxatşı çegi

vault

сақтау орны

saqtau ornı

withdraw

ақша алу

aqşa alu

Related Verbs
Қатысты етістіктер

Qatıstı etistikter

to borrow

қарызға алу

qarızğa alu

---

to cash

қолма-қол ақшаға айналдыру

qolma-qol aqşağa aynaldıru

---

to charge

ақша алу

aqşa alu

---

to deposit

ақша салу

aqşa salu

---

to endorse

қолдау

qoldau

---

to enter

тіркелу

tirkelu

---

to hold

ұстау

ustau

to insure

сақтандыру

saqtandıru

to lend

қарызға беру

qarızǧa beru

to open an account

шот ашу

şot aşu

to pay

төлеу

töleu

to save

сақтау

saqtau

to spend

жұмсау

jumsau

to transfer money

ақша аудару

aqşa audaru

to withdraw

ақша алу

aqşa alu

If you have a job, you will probably want to open a **bank account.** The two most popular **accounts** available are **checking account** and **savings account.** Banks also have many other **account** options, including **credit** lines, **money market accounts, mortgages**, etc. A **checking account** is good for your day-to-day purchases and paying your bills. You usually receive a **check card,** which works similar to a **credit card** for purchases, and a **checkbook** when you open a **checking account.** Your **check card** works like a **credit card**, however it **withdraws** money directly from your **account.** **Checks** are good for paying friends and family, bills, or anytime you have to mail a payment to someone. Most merchant's accept **checks** or **check cards** for payment, so you should not have a problem with everyday purchases with your **checking account.** You can also use your **debit card** to **withdraw cash** from **ATMs**; you will need to set up a **pin number** for **ATM transactions.** Make sure you keep track of your purchases and **withdrawals** using the **check register** because you don't want to be hit with **NSF fees.** As long as you **deposit** more **money** that you take out, you will be safe from **bank fees.** Many **banks** offer **Online Bill Pay**, making it very convenient for you to pay your bills from the comfort of your home, without ever needing to purchase a stamp. Another popular **bank account** is called a **savings account.** A **savings account** is great for long term planning. **Savings accounts** pay you **interest** on the **money** in your **account.** Different **banks** offer different **interest** rates based upon your savings habits and *balance*. This is the

account you want to put money into and only take it out in case of emergency. **Checking** and **savings accounts** work well together and are the most common types of **bank accounts** available. Many savings accounts offer **overdraft** protection for your **checking account**. If you mess up and **withdraw** too much **money**, your **savings account** funds will step in and keep you from being charged **overdraft fees. Banks** are a safe way to save and manage your money. There are many safeguards in place to protect your **accounts**. With so many features, such as **online bill pay, telephone banking,** and **direct deposit,** the smart and efficient way to manage your money is with a **bank account.**

Егер сіз жұмыс жасасаңыз, сіз **банк шотын** ашқыңыз келеді. Екі өте танымал **шоттар** бар, **ағымдағы шот** және **жинақ шоты. Банктарда** сонымен қатар, **несие** желілері, **ақша нарығы шоты, ипотекалар** сияқты тағы басқа **шот** түрлері бар. **Ағымдағы шот** сізідің күнделікті саудаңыз бен төлемдеріңізді төлеуге ыңғайлы. Әдетте сізге **банк картасы** беріледі, олар саудалар үшін **несие картасына** ұқсас жұмыс жасайды, және **чек кітапшасын** береді, ол **ағымдағы шотты** ашқан кезде беріледі. Сіздің **банк картаңыз несие картасына** ұқсайды, кез келген жағдайда да ақша сіздің **шотыңыздан тікелей** алынады. **Чектер** сіздің достарыңыз бен жанұяңыз үшін төлеуге, төлемдер төлеуге немесе төлемді пошта арқылы төлеу керек болған жағдайда ыңғайлы. Көптеген төлемге сатушылар **чектер** мен **банк картасын** қабылдайды, сондықтан сізде **ағымдағы шотыңыз** арқылы күнделікті сауда-саттық жасауда ешқандай қиын жағдай туындамауы тиіс. Сондай-ақ сіз **банкоматтан қолма-қол** ақша **алу** үшін өзіңіздің **дебет картаңызды** пайдалануыңызға болады. **Банкомат** арқылы мәмілелер үшін сіз **пин кодыңызды** анықтауыңыз керек. **Чек тіркеу қағазы** арқылы төлемдеріңіз бен ақша **алымдарыңызды** тексеріп тұрыңыз, өйткені сіз **Жеткіліксіз өтеу** алымдарын төлеуге мәжбүр болғыңыз келмейді ғой. Сіз алған **ақша** сомасынан көбірек **депозит** салып тұрсаңыз, сіз **банк алымдарынан** сақтанасыз. Көптеген **банктар Желіде төлемдер төлеуді** ұсынады, бұл сізге ешқандай мөр қойдырусыз үйде отырып төлеу ыңғайына мүмкіндік береді. Тағы басқа танымал **банк шоты** ол **жинақ шоты**. **Жинақ шоттар** ұзақ уақыт жоспарлау үшін керемет. **Жинақ шот** сізге шоттағы ақшаңыздың мөлшеріне қарай **пайыз** төлейді. Әртүрлі **банктар** сіздің төлеу әдетіңізге және теңгеріміңізге байланысты әртүрлі **пайыздық мөлшерлемелер** ұсынады. Бұл **шот** сіздің ақша салатын және тек аса қажет болған жағдайда ғана алатын шот. **Ағымдағы** және **жинақ шоты** бірге жақсы жұмыс жасайды және қолжетімді **шоттардың** ішіндегі ерекше таралған түрлері болып табылады. Көптеген **жинақ шоттар** сіздің **ағымдағы шотыңызға** овердрафт қорғанышын ұсынады. Егер сіз шектен шығып кетіп, тым көп ақша **жұмсап** қойсаңыз, сіздің **жинақ шотыңыз** төленіп, **овердрафт алымдарынан** сізді сақтап қалады. **Банктар** сіздің ақшаңызды сақтау және басқарудың қауіпсіз жолы. Сіздің **шотыңызды** сақтау үшін көптеген қорғаныштар бар. **Желіде төлемдер төлеу**, **телефон банкинг** және **тікелей депозит** сияқты көптеген ерешеліктермен сіздің ақшаңызды басқарудың ең дұрыс және әсерлі жолы ол **банк шоты**.

Eger siz jumıs jasasañız, siz **bank şotın** aşqıñız keledi. Eki öte tanımal **şottar** bar, **ağımdağı şot** jäne **jïnaq şotı. Banktarda** sonımen qatar, **nesïe** jelileri, **aqşa narığı şotı**, **ïpotekalar** sïyaqtı tağı basqa **şot** türleri bar. **Ağımdağı şot** sizidiñ kündelikti saudañız ben tölemderiñizdi töleuge ıñğaylı. Ädette sizge **bank kartası** beriledi, olar saudalar üşin **nesïe kartasına** uqsas jumıs jasaydı, jäne **çek kitapşasın** beredi, ol **ağımdağı şottı** aşqan kezde beriledi. Sizdiñ **bank kartañız nesïe kartasına** uqsaydı, kez kelgen jağdayda da aqşa sizdiñ **şotıñızdan tikeley** alınadı. **Çekter** sizdiñ dostarıñız ben januyañız üşin töleuge, tölemder töleuge nemese tölemdi poşta arqılı töleu kerek bolğan jağdayda ıñğaylı. Köptegen tölemge satuşılar **çekter** men **bank kartasın** qabıldaydı, sondıqtan sizde **ağımdağı şotıñız** arqılı kündelikti sauda-sattıq jasauda eşqanday qïın jağday tuındamauı tïis. Sonday-aq siz **bankomattan qolma-qol** aqşa **alu** üşin öziñizdiñ **debet kartañızdı** paydalanuıñızğa boladı. **Bankomat** arqılı mämileler üşin siz **pïn kodıñızdı** anıqtauıñız kerek. **Çek tirkeu qağazı** arqılı tölemderiñiz ben aqşa **alımdarıñızdı** tekserip turıñız, öytkeni siz **Jetkiliksiz öteu** alımdarın töleuge mäjbür bolğıñız kelmeydi ğoy. Siz alğan **aqşa** somasınan köbirek **depozït** salıp tursañız, siz **bank alımdarınan** saqtanasız. Köptegen **banktar Jelide tölemder töleudi** usınadı, bul sizge eşqanday mör qoydırusız üyde otırıp töleu ıñğayına mümkindik beredi. Tağı basqa tanımal **bank şotı** ol **jïnaq şotı**. **Jïnaq şottar** uzaq waqıt josparlau üşin keremet. **Jïnaq şot** sizge şottağı aqşañızdıñ mölşerine qaray **payız** töleydi. Ärtürli **banktar** sizdiñ töleu ädetiñizge jäne teñgerimiñizge baylanıstı ärtürli **payızdıq mölşerlemeler** usınadı. Bul şot sizdiñ aqşa salatın jäne tek asa qajet bolğan jağdayda ğana alatın **şot**. **Ağımdağı** jäne **jïnaq şotı** birge jaqsı jumıs jasaydı jäne qoljetimdi **şottardıñ** işindegi erekşe taralğan türleri bolıp tabıladı. Köptegen **jïnaq şottar** sizdiñ **ağımdağı şotıñızğa overdraft** qorğanışın usınadı. Eger siz şekten şığıp ketip, tım köp aqşa **jumsap** qoysañız, sizdiñ **jïnaq şotıñız** tölenip, **overdraft alımdarınan** sizdi saqtap qaladı. **Banktar** sizdiñ aqşañızdı saqtau jäne basqarudıñ qauipsiz jolı. Sizdiñ **şotıñızdı** saqtau üşin köptegen qorğanıştar bar. **Jelide tölemder töleu, telefon bankïng** jäne **tikeley depozït** sïyaqtı köptegen ereşeliktermen sizdiñ aqşañızdı basqarudıñ eñ durıs jäne äserli jolı ol **bank şotı.**

14) Holidays
14) Мерекелер
14) Merekeler

balloons

әуе шарлары

äwe şarları

calendar

күнтізбе

küntizbe

celebrate

тойлау

toylau

celebration

мереке

mereke

commemorating

еске алу

eske alu

decorations

әшекелеу

äşekeleu

family

жанұя

januya

---

feast

банкет

banket

---

federal

федералдық

federaldıq

---

festivities

той

toy

---

fireworks

отшашу

otşaşu

---

first

бірінші

birinşi

---

friends

достар

dostar

---

games

ойындар

oyındar

---

gifts

сыйлықтар

sıylıqtar

---

heros

қаһармандар

qaharmandar

---

holiday

мейрам/демалыс

meyram/demalıs

---

honor

марапат

marapat

---

national

ұлттық

ulttıq

---

parade

шеру

şeru

---

party

жиын той

jïın toy

---

picnics

пикниктер

pïknïkter

remember

есте сақтау

este saqtau

---

resolution

рұқсат беру

ruqsat beru

---

traditions

салт-дәстүрлер

salt-dästürler

American Holidays in calendar order:
Күнтізбедегі Америкалық мерекелер тізімі:
Küntizbedegi Amerïkalıq merekeler tizimi:

New Year's Day

Жаңа Жыл күні

Jaña Jıl küni

Martin Luther King Jr. Day

Кіші Мартин Лютер Кинг күні

Kişi Martïn Lyuter Kïng küni

Groundhog Day

Суыр күні

Suır küni

Valentine's Day

Әулие Валентин күні

Äulïe Valentïn küni

St. Patrick's Day

Әулие Патрик күні

Äulïe Patrïk küni

Easter

Пасха

Pasxa

April Fool's Day

Сәуірдің көңілді алдаулар күні

Säuirdiñ köñildi aldaular küni

Earth Day

Жер күні

Jer küni

Mother's Day

Аналар күні

Analar küni

Memorial Day

Еске алу күні

Eske alu küni

Father's Day

Әкелер күні

Äkeler küni

Flag Day

Ту күні

Tu küni

Independence Day/July 4th

Тәуелсіздік Күні/4 шілде

Täuelsizdik Küni/4 şilde

Labor Day

Еңбек күні

Eñbek küni

Columbus Day

Колумб күні

Kolumb küni

Halloween

Хэллоуин

Xéllouïn

Veteran's Day

Ардагерлер күні

Ardagerler küni

Election Day

Дауыс беру күні

Dauıs beru küni

Thanksgiving Day

Ризашылық күні

Rïzaşılıq küni

Christmas

Рождество

Rojdestvo

Hanukkah

Ханука күні

Xanuka küni

New Year's Eve

Жаңа Жыл қарсаңы

Jaña Jıl qarsañı

Related Verbs
Қатысты етістіктер

Qatıstı etistikter

to celebrate

тойлау

toylau

to cherish

қастерлеу

qasterleu

to commemorate

салтанатты атап өту

saltanattı atap ötu

to cook

аз әзірлеу

az äzirleu

to give

беру

beru

to go to

бару

baru

to honor

ұстану

ustanu

to observe

бақылау

baqılau

to party

тойлау

toylau

to play

ойнау

oynau

to recognize

мойындау

moyındau

to remember

есте сақтау

este saqtau

to visit

бару

baru

Many cultures and backgrounds are represented in America. With such diversity, Americans **celebrate** many **holidays** throughout the year. There are so many **holidays** on the **calendar**, there is always something to **celebrate**. In January, **New Year's Day** is a big **celebration**, but the real celebrating comes the night before; there are **fireworks** and **parties** that are broadcast all over the world. In February, we celebrate **Valentine's Day**. It is a day that most couples express their love and affection for each other with cards and gifts. In March, we celebrate **St. Patrick's Day**. Many people wear green items and celebrate Irish heritage. **Easter** is usually celebrated in April. It is a Christian **holiday**, but has also become a secular **holiday** celebrating the beginning of springtime. One of the most cherished **holidays** in America is **Mother's Day**. We honor and remember our mothers and grandmothers on this day; showering them with cards, gifts, and affection. Another big **holiday** in May is **Memorial Day**; originally declared as a day to remember our fallen **heroes** of the various branches of the United States military. It is now seen as the unofficial start of summertime and is celebrated with **picnics** and time with **family**. In June, we **celebrate Father's Day**, while it is not as popular as **Mother's Day**, the idea is the same; to **honor** and **remember** our fathers and grandfathers. In July we **celebrate Independence Day**, also known as **July 4th**. This is the day we **celebrate** our independence from England so many years ago. We **celebrate** with **fireworks** and **picnics** with **family** and **friends**. September brings **Labor Day**, the official end of summer. It was originally declared as a day to recognize the achievements of American workers in our economic successes. In October, we celebrate **Halloween**. Children dress up in their favorite costumes and go trick-or-treating for candy; many adults participate in the fun and have dress-up **parties**. In November, we celebrate **Thanksgiving Day**. It is a day to remember the early settlers to the new world and their achievements. We gather with **family** and **friends** to **feast** on turkey and other comfort-type foods. In December, we **celebrate Christmas Day. Christmas** is a Christian **holiday** that **celebrates** the birth of Jesus Christ. It is also **celebrated** by non-Christians and has many secular-type **celebrations** and **traditions**. Santa Claus visits young children on **Christmas Eve**, leaving toys and games in their stocking. **Hanukkah** is another **holiday celebrated** in December by the Jewish community; an eight-day **holiday commemorating** the rededication of the Holy Temple in Jerusalem. This is only a handful of the **holidays celebrated** by Americans. With so many **holidays**, Americans always have a reason to celebrate; so get out the **decorations**, **balloons**, and **games** and let the **festivities** begin!

Америкада көптеген мәдениеттер мен олардың тектері көрсетілген. Мұндай әр түрлілігімен Американдықтар жыл бойына көптеген **мерекелерді тойлайды**. **Күнтізбеде мерекелер** сондай көп, әрдайым **тойлайтын** бір мейрам болады. Қаңтарда **Жаңа Жыл** үлкен **мереке** болып саналады, бірақ шынайы мерекелеу бір түн бұрын басталады. Әлемнің барлық түпкірінде **отшашулар** мен **жиын тойлар** өтіп жатады. Ақпанда біздер **Валентин күнін** тойлаймыз. Бұл күні көптеген жұптар бір- біріне сезімдерін білдіріп, сыйлақтар мен ашық хаттар сыйлайды. Наурыз айында біздер **Әулие Патрик күнін** атап өтеміз. Көп адамдар жасыл түске киініп, Ирландия атамұрасын мерекелейді. **Пасха** әдеттегідей сәуір айында аталып өтіледі. Бұл христиандық **мейрам** болса да, елде бұл көктем мезгілінің келуін атап өтетін дүниежүзілік **мерекеге** айналды. **Мейрамдардың** ішіндегі ардақтысы-**Аналар күні**. Біздер аналарымыз бен әжелерімізді мақтан тұтамыз және есте сақтаймыз. Бұл күні оларды ашық хаттар, сыйлықтар мен түрлі әсерлермен жаудырамыз. Тағы бір үлкен **мереке** мамыр айында бұл **Еске алу Күні** біздің Құрама Штаттары қарулы күштерінің түрлі салаларындағы құрбан болған **қаһармандарды** еске алатын күн. Жаздың бастапқы кезін **жанұясымен пикникке** шығып мерекелеу ресми емес мерекеге айналғаны байқалады. Маусым айында біз **Әкелер Күнін** атап өтеміз, бірақ ол **Аналар Күніндей** онша танымал емес. Мақсаты бірдей –әкелеріміз бен аталарымызды **мақтан тұтып, есте сақтау**. Шілдеде біз **Тәуелсіздік Күнін мерекелейміз**, ол барлығына мәлім **4 шілде күні**. Бұл күні біз Англиядан көп жылдар бұрын тәуелсіздік алғанымызды **тойлаймыз**. Біз **достарымыз** бен **жанұяларымыздың** ортасында **отшашу** мен **пикниктер** ұйымдастырып тойлаймыз. Қыркүйек айы **Еңбек Күнін** әкеледі, ресми түрде жаздың аяқталған уақыты. Бастапқыда бұл мереке біздің экономикалық жетістіктер американдық жұмысшыларының арқасы екендігін мойындау күні деп бекітілген. Қазан айында біз **Хэллоуинды** тойламыз. Бұл күні балалар сүйікті костюмдерін киіп, тәттілер сұрауға шығады. Көптеген ересек адамдар да бұл мерекені қызықтап, костюм киінген **жиын тойлар** өткізеді. Қараша айында **Ризашылық** білдіру **Күнін** мерекелейміз. Бұл күн жаңа елге бірінші қоныс аударушыларды және олардың жетістіктерін еске алу күні болып есептеледі. Біз **жанұямыз** бен **достарымызбен** жиналып, күркетауық және тағы басқа ыңғайлы тамақтармен **банкет** өткіземіз. Желтоқсан

айында біздер **Рождество** мерекесін **тойлаймыз.**
Рождество бұл христиандардың **мерекесі**, олар бұл күні
Иса Пайғамбардың туылған күнін **мерекелейді.** Бұл
мейрам христиан емес адамдар да атап өтетін дүниелік
дәстүрлік **мейрамға** айналған. **Рождество қарсаңында**
Аяз ата кішкентай балаларға келіп, олардың
шұлықтарының ішіне сыйлықтар мен ойындар салып
кетеді. **Ханукка** желтоқсанда Жебірей тобымен
мерекеленетін тағы бір **мейрам**, бұл Иерусалимдегі киелі
ғибадатхананы қайта арнауға арналған сегізкүндік
құрмет мерекесі. Американдықтардың **тойлайтын** бұл
тек аз ғана **мерекелер** саны. **Мерекелердің** мұндай
көптігінен американдықтарға әрдайым тойлауға себеп
бар. Сондықтан **әшекейлерді, шарларды** және
ойындарды шығарып, **мерекелердің** басталуына
мүмкіндік беріңіз!

Amerïkada köptegen mädenïetter men olardıñ tekteri
körsetilgen. Munday är türliligimen Amerïkandıqtar jıl boyına
köptegen **merekelerdi toylaydı. Küntizbede merekeler**
sonday köp, ärdayım **toylaytın** bir meyram boladı. Qañtarda
Jaña Jıl ülken **mereke** bolıp sanaladı, biraq şınayı merekeleu
bir tün burın bastaladı. Älemniñ barlıq tüpkirinde **otşaşular**
men **jïın toylar** ötip jatadı. Aqpanda bizder **Valentïn künin**
toylaymız. Bul küni köptegen juptar bir-birine sezimderin
bildirip, sıylaqtar men aşıq xattar sıylaydı. Naurız ayında
bizder **Äulïe Patrïk künin** atap ötemiz. Köp adamdar jasıl
tüske kïinip, Ïrlandïya atamurasın merekeleydi. **Pasxa**
ädettegidey säuir ayında atalıp ötiledi. Bul xrïstïandıq **meyram**
bolsa da, elde bul köktem mezgiliniñ keluin atap ötetin
dünïejüzilik **merekege** aynaldı. **Meyramdardıñ** işindegi
ardaqtısı- **Analar küni.** Bizder analarımız ben äjelerimizdi

maqtan tutamız jäne este saqtaymız. Bul küni olardı aşıq xattar, sıylıqtar men türli äserlermen jaudıramız. Tağı bir ülken **mereke** mamır ayında bul **Eske alu Küni** bizdiñ Qurama Şattarı qarulı küşteriniñ türli salalarındağı qurban bolğan **qaharmandardı** eske alatın kün. Jazdıñ bastapqı kezin **januyasımen pïknïkke** şığıp merekeleu resmï emes merekege aynalğanı bayqaladı. Mausım ayında biz **Äkeler Künin** atap ötemiz, biraq ol **Analar Künindey** onşa tanımal emes. Maqsatı birdey –äkelerimiz ben atalarımızdı **maqtan tutıp**, **este saqtau**. Şildede biz **Täuelsizdik Künin merekeleymiz**, ol barlığına mälim **4 şilde küni**. Bul küni biz Anglïyadan köp jıldar burın täuelsizdik alğanımızdı **toylaymız**. Biz **dostarımız** ben **januyalarımızdıñ** ortasında **otşaşu** men **pïknïkter** uyımdastırıp toylaymız. Qırküyek ayı **Eñbek Künin** äkeledi, resmï türde jazdıñ ayaqtalğan waqıtı. Bastapqıda bul mereke bizdiñ ékonomïkalıq jetistikter amerïkandıq jumısşılarınıñ arqası ekendigin moyındau küni dep bekitilgen. Qazan ayında biz **Xéllouïndı** toylamız. Bul küni balalar süyikti kostyumderin kïip, tättiler surauğa şığadı. Köptegen eresek adamdar da bul merekeni qızıqtap, kostyum kïingen **jïın toylar** ötkizedi. Qaraşa ayında **Rïzaşılıq** bildiru **Künin** merekeleymiz. Bul kün jaña elge birinşi qonıs audaruşılardı jäne olardıñ jetistikterin eske alu küni bolıp esepteledi. Biz **januyamız** ben **dostarımızben** jïnalıp, kürketauıq jäne tağı basqa ıñğaylı tamaqtarmen **banket** ötkizemiz. Jeltoqsan ayında bizder **Rojdestvo** merekesin toylaymız. Rojdestvo bul xrïstïandardıñ **merekesi**, olar bul küni Ïsa Payğambardıñ tuılğan künin **merekeleydi**. Bul **meyram** xrïstïan emes adamdar da atap ötetin dünïelik dästürlik **meyramğa** aynalğan. **Rojdestvo qarsañında** Ayaz ata kişkentay balalarğa kelip, olardıñ şulıqtarınıñ işine sıylıqtar men oyındar salıp ketedi. **Xanukka** jeltoqsanda Jebirey tobımen **merekelenetin** tağı bir **meyram**, bul Ïerusalïmdegi kïeli ğïbadatxananı qayta arnauğa arnalğan segizkündik **qurmet merekesi**. Amerïkandıqtardıñ **toylaytın** bul tek az ğana **merekeler** sanı. **Merekelerdiñ** munday köptiginen amerïkandıqtarğa ärdayım toylauğa sebep bar. Sondıqtan **äşekeylerdi**, **şarlardı** jäne **oyındardı** şığarıp, **merekelerdiñ** bastaluına mümkindik beriñiz!

15) Traveling
15) Саяхаттау
15) Sayaxattau

airport

әуежай

äwejay

---

backpack

жолдорба

joldorba

---

baggage

жүк

jük

---

boarding pass

отыратын талон

otıratın talon

---

business class

бизнес класс

bïznes klass

---

bus station

автобус стансасы

avtobus stansası

---

carry-on

қол жүк

qol jük

check-in

тіркелу

tirkelu

coach

автобус

avtobus

cruise

теңіз саяхаты

teñiz sayaxatı

depart/departure

кету/шығу

ketu/şığu

destination

баратын жер

baratın jer

excursion

экскурсия

ékskursïya

explore

зерттеу

zertteu

first class

бірінші класс

birinşi klass

---

flight

ұшу

uşu

---

flight attendant

жолсерік

jolserik

---

fly

ұшу

uşu

---

guide

гид

gïd

---

highway

тас жол

tas jol

---

hotel

мейманхана

meymanxana

---

inn

қонақ үй

qonaq üy

---

journey

сапар

sapar

---

land

жер

jer

---

landing

жерге қону

jerge qon

---

lift-off

көтерілу

köterilu

---

luggage

жүк

Jük

---

map

карта

karta

---

move

қозғалу

qozğalu

---

motel

мотель

motel'

---

passenger

жолаушы

jolauşı

---

passport

паспорт

pasport

---

pilot

ұшқыш

uşqış

---

port

порт

port

---

postcard

ашық хат

aşıq xat

---

rail

рельс

rel's

---

railway

темір жол

temir jol

---

red-eye

түнгі сапар

tüngi sapar

---

reservations

орын сақтау

orın saqtau

---

resort

шипажай

şïpajay

---

return

қайту

qaytu

---

road

жол

jol

---

roam

серуендеу

seruendeu

---

room

бөлме

bölme

---

route

бағдар

bağdar

---

safari

сафари

safarï

---

sail

желкен

jelken

seat

орын

orın

sightseeing

көрікті жерлерді аралау

körikti jerlerdi aralau

souvenir

кәдесый

kädesıy

step

қадам

qadam

suitcase

шабадан

şabadan

take off

ұшу

uşu

tour

тур

tur

tourism

туризм

turïzm

tourist

саяхатшы

sayaxatşı

traffic

қозғалыс

qozğalıs

trek

саяхат

sayaxat

travel

саяхат

sayaxat

travel agent

турагент

turagent

trip

сапар

sapar

vacation

демалыс

demalıs

voyage

саяхат

sayaxat

Modes of Transportation
Көлік түрлері

Kölik türleri

---

airplane/plane

ұшақ

uşaq

---

automobile

автокөлік

avtokölik

---

balloon

әуе шары

äwe şarı

---

bicycle

велосипед

velosïped

---

boat

қайық

qayıq

---

bus

автобус

avtobus

---

canoe

каноэ

kanoé

---

car

автокөлік

avtokölik

---

ferry

паром

parom

---

motorcycle

мотоцикл

motocïkl

---

motor home

жылжымалы үй

jıljımalı üy

---

ship

кеме

keme

---

subway

метро

metro

---

taxi

такси

taksï

---

train
поезд
poezd

van
фургон
furgon

Hotels
Мейманханалар
Meymanxanalar

accessible
қолжетімді
qoljetimdi

airport shuttle
перрондық автобус
perrondıq avtobus

all-inclusive
кешенді
keşendi

amenities
жайлылық
jaylılıq

balcony
балкон
balkon

bathroom

ванна бөлмесі

vanna bölmesi

beach

жағажай

jağajay

beds

кереуеттер

kereuetter

bed and breakfast

таңғы ас ұсынатын қонақ үй

tañğı as usınatın qonaq üy

bellboy/bellhop

шабарман

şabarman

bill

шот

şot

breakfast

таңғы ас

tañğı as

business center

бизнес орталығы

bïznes ortalığı

cable/satellite tv
кабельді/спутниктік теледидар
kabel'di/sputnïktik teledïdar

charges (in-room)
төлемдер
tölemder

check-in
тіркелу
tirkelu

check-out
бөлмені босату
bölmeni bosatu

concierge
есікші
esikşi

Continental breakfast
континенталдық таңғы ас
kontïnentaldıq tañğı as

corridors (interior)
дәліздер
dälizder

doorman
есікші
esikşi

double bed

екікісілік кереует

ekikisilik kereuet

---

double room

екі адамдық бөлме

eki adamdıq bölme

---

elevator

лифт

lïft

---

exercise/fitness room

фитнес зал

fïtnes zal

---

extra bed

қосымша кереует

qosımşa kereuet

---

floor

еден

eden

---

front desk

қабылдау орны

qabıldau ornı

---

full breakfast

толық таңғы ас

tolıq tañğı as

---

gift shop

сыйлықтар дүкені

sıylıqtar dükeni

guest

қонақ

qonaq

guest laundry

кір жуатын бөлме

kir juatın bölme

hair dryer

фен

fen

high-rise

биік ғимарат

bïik ğïmarat

hotel

мейманхана

meymanxana

housekeeping

жинастыру

jïnastıru

information desk

анықтама беретін орын

anıqtama beretin orın

inn

қонақ үй

qonaq üy

in-room

бөлмеде

bölmede

internet

ғаламтор

ğalamtor

iron/ironing board

үтік/үтіктеу тақтасы

ütik/ütikteu taqtası

key

кілт

Kilt

king bed

кереует

kereuet

lobby

лобби

lobbï

local calls

жергілікті қоңыраулар

jergilikti qoñıraular

lounge

зал

zal

---

luggage

жүк

Jük

---

luxury

молшылық

molşılıq

---

maid

қызметші әйел

qızmetşi äyel

---

manager

менеджер

menedjer

---

massage

массаж

massaj

---

meeting room

конференц-зал

konferenc-zal

---

microwave

қысқа толқынды пеш

qısqa tolqındı peş

---

mini-bar

шағын-бар

şağın-bar

---

motel

мотель

motel'

---

newspaper

газет

gazet

---

newsstand

газет киоскісі

gazet kïoskisi

---

non-smoking

темекі шекпейтін адамдарға

temeki şekpeytin adamdarğa

---

pets/no pets

үй жануарларымен/үй жануарларынсыз

üy januarlarımen/üy januarlarınsız

---

pool - indoor/outdoor

бассейн ішкі/сыртқы

basseyn işki/sırtqı

---

porter

есікші

esikşi

---

queen bed

кереует

kereuet

parking

көлік тұрағы

kölik turağı

receipt

түбіртек

tübirtek

reception desk

қабылдау бөлімшесі

qabıldau bölimşesi

refrigerator (in-room)

тоңазытқыш (бөлмеде)

toñazıtqış (bölmede)

reservation

орын сақтау

orın saqtau

restaurant

мейрамхана

meyramxana

room

бөлме

bölme

room number
бөлменің нөмірі
bölmeniñ nömiri

---

room service
бөлме қызметі
bölme qızmeti

---

safe (in-room)
темірсандық (бөлмеде)
temirsandıq (bölmede)

---

service charge
қызмет төлемі
qızmet tölemi

---

shower
душ
duş

---

single room
бір адамдық бөлме
bir adamdıq bölme

---

suite
люкс
lyuks

---

tax
салық
salıq

---

tip

шайпұл

şaypul

---

twin bed

қос кереует

qos kereuet

---

vacancy/ no vacancy

бос жұмыс орындары /бос жұмыс орындары жоқ

bos jumıs orındarı /bos jumıs orındarı joq

---

wake-up call

ояту қоңырауы

oyatu qoñıraui

---

whirlpool/hot tub

джакузи

djakuzï

---

wireless high-speed internet

сымсыз жылдам ғаламтор

sımsız jıldam ğalamtor

Related Verbs
Қатысты етістіктер

Qatıstı etistikter

to arrive

келу

kelu

---

to ask

сұрау

surau

to buy

сатып алу

satıp alu

to catch a flight

рейске үлгеру

reyske ülgeru

to change

айырбастау

ayırbastau

to drive

айдау

aydau

to find

табу

tabu

to fly

ұшу

Uşu

to land

жерге қону

jerge qonu

to make a reservation

орынды сақтату

orındı saqtatu

---

to pack

киім жинау

kïim jïnau

---

to pay

төлеу

töleu

---

to recommend

ұсыныс жасау

usınıs jasau

---

to rent

жалдау

jaldau

---

to see

көру

köru

---

to stay

қалу

qalu

---

to take off

ұшу

uşu

---

to travel

саяхаттау

sayaxattau

---

to swim

жүзу

jüzu

Michael is young and adventurous and loves to **travel**; ever since he was a little boy, he has enjoyed the excitement of **traveling**. Whether he **travels** by **boat**, **car**, or **plane**; he always has a great time. Michael has **traveled** all over the world on **vacation**. Once, he took a **bus** from Florida to California, just to say he had done so. His wife enjoys **traveling** with Michael; however, she is not an adventurous person. She likes to **vacation** in nice, quiet places. She prefers an easy **trip** that does not require **layovers** or complicated **itineraries**. Her favorite **destination** is Hawaii, so Michael decided to take her there for their anniversary. They made their **reservations** and took a **plane** from California to Hawaii; or so they thought. That is where this **journey** begins. They bought **tickets** on the **red-eye flight** to get an early start on **vacation**. They arrived at the **airport**, got their **luggage checked-in** and with their **carry-on bags** in hand, they headed towards the **concourse**, ready to **fly** away into the sunset! They were in such a hurry to get to their **destination**; they unknowingly **boarded** the wrong **plane**. They both slept during the **flight** and when they arrived, they both felt something was not quite right; they had traveled to **Alaska**! They checked with their **travel agency** and found out there were no **flights** leaving that **airport** until the next morning. Determined to get to their **vacation** in Hawaii, the couple decided to do whatever it took to get there! They took a **ferry** to the nearest **car** rental location and decided to **drive** as much of the way as possible; they would figure the rest out later. They picked up a **map** and headed on their way. They figured they would get to do some **sightseeing** along the way, if nothing else. It was a long **drive**; they drove for hundreds of miles until they just couldn't drive anymore, so they stopped at a **hotel** to get some rest. The next morning, they **checked-out** of their **hotel room** and continued driving. Their **travel agent** called them and said that they had **coach tickets** the next morning, leaving out of LAX **airport**; they just had to be there in time. The couple made it to the **airport** with just ten minutes to spare! They finally **boarded** their **flight**, on their way to Hawaii. When they arrived at the **airport**, they were so relieved to finally be on **vacation**! They took a **shuttle** to the **resort** and finally were able to enjoy a nice, relaxing **vacation**. Of all Michael's **travels**, this was the most adventurous one yet!

Майкл жас әрі шытырман оқиғаларға үйір және **саяхаттағанды** жақсы көреді. Ол кішкентай бала болған кезден бастап саяхаттаудың толқуын қызықтайтын. Ол **қайық, автокөлік** немесе **ұшақпен** саяхаттаса да, уақытты тамаша өткізетін. Майкл **демалысында** әлемнің барлық жеріне **саяхаттады**. Бірде ол Флоридадан Колифорнияға **автобуспен** барды, тек солай бардым деп айта алу үшін ғана. Оның зайыбы Майклмен **саяхаттағанды** ұнатады. Бірақ ол онша шытырман адам емес. Ол тыныш, жайлы жерде **демалғанды** ұнатады. Ол **ұшақтың ұшуы кейінге қалдырулар** мен **қиын бағдарларға** қарағанда, жеңіл **сапарды** қалайды. Оның сүйікті **баратын жері** Гавайи, сондықтан Майкл өздерінің жылдық мерекелеріне оны сонда алып баруды шешті. Олар өздерінің **орындарын сақтаттырды** және Гавайидан Колифорнияға **ұшақпен** ұшты, немесе олар солай ойлады. Осы жерден нағыз **саяхат** басталады. Олар демалысты ерте бастау үшін **билетті түнгі сапарға** алды. Олар **әуежайға** келіп, **тіркелген жүктері** мен қолдарына **қол жүктерін** алды да, күнбатысқа қарай **ұшуға** дайын бола, **есікшіге** беттеді. Олар **баратын жерлеріне** асыққаны сонша, басқа **ұшаққа отырғанын** байқамады. **Ұшу** кезінде олар екеуі де ұйықтап шықты. Бірақ тұрған соң, бір нәрсе бұрыс екенін түсінді. Олар **Аляскаға** саяхаттап бара жатыр екен! Олар өздерінің **турагентімен** тексеріп шықты, бірақ ертеңге дейін ешқандай ұшақ ұшпайтындығы анықталды. Олар **демалысын** Гавайида өткізу үшін міндетті түрде онда жетуді шешті. Олар **пароммен** ең жақын **автокөліктерді** жалға беретін жерге жетіп, қанша жер жүруге мүмкін болғанша автокөлік **айдауға** және кейін демалатындарын шешті. Олар барар жолға **карта** алды. Олар тым құрғанда, жолдағы **көрікті жерлерді** аралаймыз деп ойлады. Бұл өте ұзақ **айдау** болды. Ол бірнеше жүз миля айдаған соң, шаршап, демалу үшін бір **мейманханаға** келіп тоқтады. Таңертең олар мейманханадағы **бөлмелерін тапсырып**, әрі қарай айдауды жалғастырды. Олардың **турагенті** қоңырау соқты және Лос Анджелес Халықаралық **әуежайынан** жүретін **автобусқа билет** бар екендігін айтты, оларға тек уақытында сонда болу керек еді. Бұл жұп үнемдеу үшін он минут ішінде **әуежайға** келіп үлгерді! Нәтижесінде олар Гавайиға баратын **ұшаққа отырды**. Олар **әуежайға** келгенде, түбінде **демалыстарына** жеткендеріне қуанды! Олар **шипажайға** жету үшін **жүрдек поезына** отырды.

Сөйтіп, жақсы, рахаттанатын **демалыс** өткізеді. Майклдың барлық **саяхатынан**, ең шытырман саяхаты осы еді.

Maykl jas äri şıtırman oqïğalarğa üyir jäne **sayaxattağandı** jaqsı köredi. Ol **qayıq**, **avtokölik** nemese **uşaqpen** sayaxattasa, ol waqıttı tamaşa ötkizetin. Maykl **demalısında** älemniñ barlıq jerine **sayaxattady**. Birde ol Florïdadan Kolïfornïyağa **avtobuspen** bardı, tek solay bardım dep ayta alu üşin ğana. Onıñ zayıbı Mayklmen **sayaxattağandı** unatadı. Biraq ol onşa şıtırman adam emes. Ol tınış, jaylı jerde **demalğandı** unatadı. Ol **uşaqtıñ uşuı keyinge qaldırular** men **qïin bağdarlarğa** qarağanda, jeñil **sapardı** qalaydı. Onıñ süyikti **baratın jeri** Gavayï, sondıqtan Maykl özderiniñ jıldıq merekelerine onı sonda alıp barudı şeşti. Olar özderiniñ **orındarın saqtattırdı** jäne Gavayïdan Kolïfornïyağa **uşaqpen** uştı, nemese olar solay oyladı. Osı jerden nağız **sayaxat** bastaladı. Olar demalıstı erte bastau üşin **bïletti tüngi saparğa** aldı. Olar **äwejayğa** kelip, **tirkelgen jükteri** men qoldarına **qol jükterin** aldı da, künbatısqa qaray **uşuğa** dayın bola, **esikşige** bettedi. Olar **baratın jerlerine** asıqqanı sonşa, basqa **uşaqqa otırğanın** bayqamadı. **Uşu** kezinde olar ekeui de uyıqtap şıqtı. Biraq turğan soñ, bir närse burıs ekenin tüsindi. Olar **Alyaskağa** sayaxattap bara jatır eken! Olar özderiniñ **turagentimen** tekserip şıqtı, biraq erteñge deyin eşqanday uşaq uşpaytındığı anıqtaldı. Olar **demalısın** Gavayïda ötkizu üşin mindetti türde onda jetudi şeşti. Olar **parommen** eñ jaqın **avtökölikterdi** jalğa beretin jerge jetip, qanşa jer jüruge mümkin bolğanşa avtokölik **aydauğa** jäne keyin demalatındarın şeşti. Olar barar jolğa **karta** aldı. Olar tım qurğanda, joldağı **körikti jerlerdi** aralaymız dep oyladı. Bul öte uzaq **aydau** boldı. Ol birneşe jüz mïlya aydağan soñ, şarşap, demalu üşin bir **meymanxanağa** kelip toqtadı. Tañerteñ olar meymanxanadağı **bölmelerin**

tapsırıp, äri qaray aydaudı jalğastırdı. Olardıñ **turagenti**
qoñırau soqtı jäne Los Andjeles Xalıqaralıq **äwejayınan** jüretin
avtobusqa bïlet bar ekendigin ayttı, olarğa tek waqıtında
sonda bolu kerek edi. Bul jup ünemdeu üşin on mïnut işinde
äwejayğa kelip ülgerdi! Nätïjesinde olar Gavayïğa baratın
uşaqqa otırdı. Olar **äwejayğa** kelgende, tübinde
demalıstarına jetkenderine quandı! Olar **şïpajayğa** jetu üşin
jürdek poezına otırdı. Söytip, jaqsı, raxattanatın **demalıs**
ötkizedi. Maykldıñ barlıq **sayaxatınan**, eñ şıtırman sayaxatı osı
edi.

16) School
16) Мектеп
16) Mektep

arithmetic

есеп

esep

assignment

тапсырма

tapsırma

atlas

атлас

atlas

backpack

арқа қоржын

arqa qorjın

binder

мұқаба

muqaba

blackboard

тақта

taqta

book

кітап

kitap

bookbag

кітап қоржыны

kitap qorjını

bookcase

кітап шкафі

kitap şkafi

bookmark

белгі бауы

belgi bauı

calculator

калькулятор

kal'kulyator

calendar

күнтізбе

küntizbe

chalk

бор

bor

chalkboard

борға арналған тақтасы

borğa arnalğan taqtası

chart

кесте

keste

---

class clown

сынып сайықмазағы

sınıp sayıqmazağı

---

classmate

сыныптас

sınıptas

---

classroom

сынып

sınıp

---

clipboard

ауыстыру буфері

auıstıru buferi

---

coach

бапкер

bapker

---

colored pencils

түрлі түсті қарындаштар

türli tüsti qarındaştar

---

compass

компас

kompas

---

composition book

қалың дәптер

qalıñ däpter

computer

компьютер

komp'yuter

construction paper

қалың қағаз

qalıñ qağaz

crayons

қарындаш

qarındaş

desk

парта

parta

dictionary

сөздік

sözdik

diploma

диплом

dïplom

dividers

циркуль

cïrkul'

dormitory

жатақхана

jataqxana

dry-erase board

құрғақ өшірілетін тақта

qurğaq öşiriletin taqta

easel

мольберт

mol'bert

encyclopedia

энциклопедия

éncïklopedïya

english

ағылшын тілі

ağılşın tili

eraser

өшіргіш

öşirgiş

exam

емтихан

emtïxan

experiment

тәжірибе

täjirïbe

flash cards

флэш карталары

fléş kartaları

folder

папка

papka

geography

география

geografiya

globe

жер шары

jer şarı

glossary

глоссарий

glossarïy

glue

желім

jelim

gluestick

қарындаш желім

qarındaş jelim

grades, A, B, C, D, F, passing, failing

бағалар, 5,4,3,2,1, тапсыру, құлау

bağalar, 5,4,3,2,1, tapsıru, qulau

gym

спортзал

sportzal

---

headmaster

директор

dïrektor

---

highlighter

маркер

marker

---

history

тарих

tarïx

---

homework

үй жұмысы

üy jumısı

---

ink

сия

sïya

---

janitor

сыпырушы

sıpıruşı

Kindergarten

бала-бақша

bala -baqşa

---

keyboard

пернетақта

pernetaqta

---

laptop

ноутбук

noutbuk

---

lesson

сабақ

sabaq

---

library

кітапхана

kitapxana

---

librarian

кітапханашы

kitapxanaşı

---

lockers

локерлер

lokerler

---

lunch

түскі ас

tüski as

---

lunch box/bag

түскі ас қорабы/қоржын

tüski as qorabı/qorjın

---

map
карта
karta

markers
маркерлер
markerler

math
математика
matematïka

notebook
дәптер
däpter

notepad
блокнот
bloknot

office
кеңсе
keñse

paper
қағаз
qağaz

paste
паста
pasta

pen

қалам

qalam

---

pencil

қарындаш

qarındaş

---

pencil case

пенал

penal

---

pencil sharpener

ұштағыш

uştağış

---

physical education/PE

дене шынықтыру

dene şınıqtıru

---

portfolio

портфолио

portfolio

---

poster

плакат

plakat

---

principal

директор

direktor

---

professor

профессор

professor

---

project

жоба

joba

---

protractor

транспортир

transportïr

---

pupil

оқушы

oquşı

---

question

сұрақ

suraq

---

quiz

білімін сынау сұрақтары

bilimin sınau suraqtarı

---

read

оқу

oqu

---

reading

оқу

oqu

---

recess

үзіліс

üzilis

---

ruler

сызғыш

sızğış

---

science

ғылым

ğılım

---

scissors

қайшы

qayşı

---

secretary

хатшы

xatşı

---

semester

тоқсан

toqsan

---

stapler

степлер

stepler

---

student

студент

student

---

tape

таспа

taspa

teacher

мұғалім

muğalim

test

тест

test

thesaurus

тақырыптық сөздік

taqırıptıq sözdik

vocabulary

сөздік

sözdik

watercolors

акварель

akvarel'

whiteboard

тақта

taqta

write

жазу

jazu

Related Verbs
Қатысты етістіктер
Qatıstı etistikter

to answer
жауап беру
jauap beru

to ask
сұрау
surau

to draw
сурет салу
suret salu

to drop out
оқуды тастау
oqudı tastau

to erase
өшіру
öşiru

to fail
құлау
qulau

to learn
үйрену
üyrenu

to pass

тапсыру

tapsıru

to play

ойнау

oynau

to read

оқу

oqu

to register

тіркелу

tirkelu

to show up

көріну

körinu

to sign up

қол қою

qol qoyu

to study

оқу

oqu

to teach

оқыту

oqıtu

to test

тексеру

tekseru

---

to think

ойлау

oylau

---

to write

жазу

jazu

Heather is five years old and has always enjoyed being home with her mom every day. She heard that she would be starting **school** soon and was nervous about it. Summer was coming to an end and Heather was really starting to get anxious about the start of the **school** year. This will be her first and she is unsure about what to expect. She was excited, yet nervous to leave her mom all day. Her mom took her **school supply** shopping on the Saturday before school was to start. She had her list of **school supplies** and was very overwhelmed by all the things in the store. There are so many things on the list, she doesn't know where to start; **crayons**, **paper**, **markers**, **glue**, and more! Heather's mom told her she would need something to put all this stuff in, so she picked out a nice **backpack** with her favorite cartoon cat on it; it also had a matching **lunch bag**! Her mom told her she would also need to get some new clothes because every little girl needs new clothes for the first day of **school**. On the way home from shopping, Heather questioned her mom about **school;** she was getting very excited because she wondered what she would be doing with all this stuff! The first day of **school** finally came and Heather's mom took her to register for the first day of **Kindergarten**. The first stop was the **office**, she met a very nice lady, the **school secretary**, and she also met a handsome gentleman who said he was the **principal** of the **school**. She wasn't sure what that meant, but he must be important. Once everything was settled in the **office**, her mom took her to her new **classroom**. When she walked in, she couldn't believe her eyes; it was amazing! There was a big **chalkboard** on the wall, rows of **desks**, colorful **charts** and **maps**, even some games and **books**. She really likes games and **books**, so she started to relax a bit. Then, she saw her new **teacher**; she was a nice lady, smiling and being very polite. Heather then realized she would be okay. She sent her mom on her way and told her she would see her this afternoon after **school**. She was ready to learn to **read** and **write**, do **math** and **science**; she was not nervous anymore! That day she made several new friends and really like her **teacher**. They had **English** and **Math**; she even got to paint using her new **watercolors**. Heather decided she loved **school** and wanted to come back every day!

Хизер бес жаста және күнде анасымен үйде болғанды ұнатады. Ол жақын арада **мектепке** баратынын естіді және бұл жөнінде қобалжыды. Жаздың аяғы да жақындады және Хизер **мектеп** жылының басталғанына шынайы мазасыздана бастады. Бұл оның өмірінде бірінші рет болып жатқандықтан, ол не күтетінін де білмеді. Ол қуанышты болды, бірақ күні бойы анасын көрмейтініне абыржыды. Оның анасы мектеп басталмас бұрын, сенбі күні оған барлық **мектеп керек-жарақтарымен** қамтамасыз етті. Ол **мектеп керек-жарақтарының** тізімін қолына алып, дүкен ішіндегі көптеген заттарға таң қалды. Тізім ішінде сонша көп зат болғандықтан, ол қай жерден бастарын білмеді: **қарындаштар**, **қағаздар**, **маркерлер**, **желім** және одан да көп заттар! Хизердің анасы оған бұл заттардың бәрін салатын зат керек деп, бетінде оның сүйікті мультфильміндегі мысықтың суреті бар әдемі **арқа қоржынын** алды. Мұнда сонымен қатар, **түскі асқа** арналған **қап** болды! Оның анасы оған біршама жаңа киім алу керектігін айтты, өйткені әрбір кішкентай қыз **мектепке** бірінші күні жаңа киіммен барады. Саудадан үйге келе жатқан жолда Хизер анасынан **мектеп** туралы сұрақтар қойды. Ол өте қобалжып тұрды, өйткені ол барлық мына заттармен не істейтінін ойлап таңданды! **Мектепке** баратын бірінші күн де нәтижесінде келді және Хизердің анасы оны **Бала- бақшаның** бірінші күніне тіркеуге алып келді. Олардың бірінші келген жері **кеңсе** болды, ол өте жақсы бір ханымды кездестірді, ол **мектеп хатшысы** еді, содан соң, ол бір сұлу мырзаны кездестірді, ол **мектеп директоры** екендігін айтты. Бұл сөздің мағынасын түсінбеді, алайда бұл маңызды адам болуы тиіс. **Кеңседе** барлық мәселелер шешілген соң, Хизердің анасы оны оның жаңа **сыныбына** апарды. Ол сыныптың ішіне кіргенде, ол өз көздеріне сенбеді. Ол жер тамаша еді! Мұнда жарда үлкен **тақта** ілініп тұрды, **парталардың** қатары, түрлі түсті **кестелер** мен **карталар**, тіпті бірнеше **кітаптар** мен ойындар болды. Ол ойындар мен **кітаптарды** қатты ұнататын, сондықтан ол өзін біршама еркін сезінді. Кейін ол өзінің жаңа **мұғалімін** көрді, ол жақсы ханым болатын, ол күлімсіреп, өте сыпайы болды. Хизер барлығы жақсы болатынын түсінді және анасын шығарып салып, оған **мектептен** соң түстен кейін кездесеміз деді. Ол **оқуды**, **жазуды**, **матетамика** шығаруды, **ғылымды** зерттеуді үйренуге дайын болды.

Ол ендігі қобалжымады. Бұл күні ол бірнеше жаңа достар тапты және өзінің **мұғалімін** сондай ұнатты. Оларда **ағылшын тілі** мен **математика** сабақтары болды. Ол тіпті өзінің жаңа **акварелін** пайдаланып, сурет салды. Хизер **мектепті** ұнатты және мұнда күнде баруын қалады!

Xïzer bes jasta jäne künde anasımen üyde bolğandı unatadı. Ol jaqın arada **mektepke** baratının estidi jäne bul jöninde qobaljidı. Jazdıñ ayağı da jaqındadı jäne Xïzer **mektep** jılınıñ bastalğanına şınayı mazasızdana bastadı. Bul onıñ ömirinde birinşi ret bolıp jatqandıqtan, ol ne kütetinin de bilmedi. Ol quanıştı boldı, biraq küni boyı anasın körmeytinine abırjıdı. Onıñ anası mektep bastalmas burın, senbi küni oğan barlıq **mektep kerek-jaraqtarımen** qamtamasız etti. Ol **mektep kerek-jaraqtarınıñ** tizimin qolına alıp, düken işindegi köptegen zattarğa tañ qaldı. Tizim işinde sonşa köp zat bolğandıqtan, ol qay jerden bastarın bilmedi: **qarındaştar**, **qağazdar**, **markerler**, **jelim** jäne odan köp zattar! Xïzerdiñ anası oğan bul zattardıñ bärin salatın zat kerek dep, betinde onıñ süyikti mul'tfïl'mindegi mısıqtıñ sureti bar ädemi **arqa qorjının** aldı. Munda sonımen qatar, **tüski asqa** arnalğan **qap** boldı! Onıñ anası oğan birşama jaña kïim alu kerektigin ayttı, öytkeni ärbir kişkentay qız **mektepke** birinşi küni jaña kïimmen baradı. Saudadan üyge kele jatqan jolda Xïzer anasınan **mektep** turalı suraqtar qoydı. Ol öte qobaljıp turdı, öytkeni ol barlıq mına zattarmen ne isteytinin oylap tañdandı! **Mektepke** baratın birinşi kün de nätïjesinde keldi jäne Xïzerdiñ anası onı **Bala- baqşanıñ** birinşi künine tirkeuge alıp keldi. Olardıñ birinşi kelgen jeri **keñse** boldı, ol öte jaqsı bir xanımdı kezdestirdi, ol **mektep xatşısı** edi, sodan soñ, ol bir sulu mırzanı kezdestirdi, ol **mektep direktory** ekendigin ayttı. Bul cözdiñ mağınasın tüsinbedi, alayda bul mañızdı adam boluı tiis. **Keñsede** barlıq mäseleler şeşilgen soñ, Xïzerdiñ anası onı onıñ jaña **sınıbına** apardı. Ol sınıptıñ işine kirgende, ol öz közderine senbedi. Ol jer tamaşa edi! Munda jarda ülken **taqta** ilinip turdı, **partalardıñ** qatarı, türli tüsti **kesteler** men **kartalar**, tipti birneşe **kitaptar** men oyındar boldı. Ol oyındar men **kitaptardı** qattı unatatın, sondıqtan ol özin birşama erkin sezindi. Keyin ol öziniñ jaña **muğalimin** kördi, ol jaqsı xanım bolatın, ol külimsirep, öte sıpayı boldy. Xïzer barlığı jaqsı bolatının tüsindi jäne anasın şığarıp salıp, oğan **mektepten** soñ tüsten keyin kezdesemiz dedi. Ol **oqudı**, **jazudı**, **matetamïka** şığarudı, **ğılımdı** zertteudi üyrenuge dayın boldı. Ol endigi qobaljımadı. Bul küni ol birneşe jaña dostar taptı jäne öziniñ **muğalimin** sonday unattı. Olarda **ağılşın tili** men **matematïka** sabaqtarı boldı. Ol tipti öziniñ jaña **akvarelin** paydalanıp, suret saldı. Xïzer **mektepti** unattı jäne munda künde baruın qaladı!

17) Hospital
17) Аурухана
17) Auruxana

ache

ауыру

auıru

acute

өткір

ötkir

allergy/allergic

аллергия/аллергиялық

allergïya/allergïyalıq

ambulance

жедел жәрдем

jedel järdem

amnesia

амнезия

amnezïya

amputation

ампутация

amputacïya

anaemia

қаназдық

qanazdıq

---

anesthesiologist

анестезиолог

anestezïolog

---

antibiotics

антибиотиктер

antïbïotïkter

---

anti-depressant

антидепрессант

antïdepressant

---

appointment

ем белгілеу

em belgileu

---

arthritis

артрит

artrït

---

asthma

демікпе

demikpe

---

bacteria

бактерия

bakterïya

---

bedsore

ұзақ жатқаннан ойылған жер

uzaq jatqannan oyılğan jer

biopsy

биопсия

bïopsïya

blood

қан

qan

blood count

қан талдауы

qan taldauı

blood donor

донор

donor

blood pressure

қан қысымы

qan qısımı

blood test

қан тексеру

qan tekseru

bone

сүйек

süyek

brace

қапсырма

qapsırma

bruise

көгерген жер

kögergen jer

Caesarean section (C-section)

Кесарев кесуі

Kesarev kesui

cancer

обыр

obır

cardiopulmonary resuscitation (CPR)

жүректі-өкпелі реанимация

jürekti-ökpeli reanïmacïya

case

оқиға

oqïğa

cast

гипс

gïps

chemotherapy

химиотерапия

xïmïoterapïya

coroner

қан тамыры

qan tamırı

---

critical

ауыр

auır

---

crutches

балдақтар

baldaqtar

---

cyst

сарысулы ісік

sarısulı isik

---

deficiency

тапшылық

tapşılıq

---

dehydrated

құрғаған

qurğağan

---

diabetes

сусамыр

susamır

---

diagnosis

диагноз

dïagnoz

---

dietician

диета дәрігері

dïeta därigeri

---

disease

ауру

auru

---

doctor

дәрігер

däriger

---

emergency

төтенше жағдай

tötenşe jağday

---

emergency room (ER)

шапшаң жәрдем ету бөлмесі

şapşañ järdem etu bölmesi

---

exam

емтихан

emtïxan

---

fever

дене қызуы көтерілу

dene qızuı köterilu

---

flu (influenza)

тұмау

tumau

---

fracture

сынық

sınıq

heart attack

жүрек ұстау

jürek ustau

hematologist

гематолог

gematolog

hives

есекжем

esekjem

hospital

аурухана

auruxana

illness

ауру

auru

imaging

бейнелеу

beyneleu

immunization

имунитеттеу

ïmunïtetteu

infection

инфекция

ïnfekcïya

Intensive Care Unit (ICU)

интенсивті терапия бөлімі

ïntensïvti terapïya bölimi

IV

көктамырдың ішіне егу

köktamırdıñ işine egu

---

laboratory (lab)

лабаратория

labaratorïya

---

life support

тіршілікті қамтамасыз ету

tirşilikti qamtamasız etu

---

mass

масса

massa

---

medical technician

медициналық техника маманы

medïcïnalıq texnïka mamanı

---

neurosurgeon

нейрохирург

neyroxïrurg

---

nurse
медбике
medbïke

operating room (OR)
операциялық бөлме
operacïyalıq bölme

operation
операция
operacïya

ophthalmologist
офтальмолог
oftal'molog

orthopedic
ортопедиялық
ortopedïyalıq

pain
ауыру
auıru

patient
емделуші
emdeluşi

pediatrician
педиатр
pedïatr

pharmacist

фармацевт

farmacevt

pharmacy

дәріхана

därixana

physical Therapist

физиотерапевт

fïzïoterapevt

physician

дәрігер

däriger

poison

у

u

prescription

дәріқағаз

däriqağaz

psychiatrist

психиатр

psïxïatr

radiologist

радиолог

radïolog

resident

тұрғын

turğın

---

scan

қарау

qarau

---

scrubs

хирург костюмі

xïrurg kostyumi

---

shots

егу

egu

---

side effects

жанама әсері

janama äseri

---

specialist

маман

maman

---

stable

тұрақты

turaqtı

---

surgeon

хирург

xïrurg

---

symptoms

белгілер

belgiler

---

therapy

терапия

terapïya

---

treatment

емдеу

emdeu

---

vein

көктамыр

köktamır

---

visiting hours

қабылдау уақыты

qabıldau waqıtı

---

visitor

келуші

keluşi

---

wheelchair

мүгедектік кресло

mügedektik kreslo

---

x-ray

рентген

rentgen

Related Verbs
Қатысты етістіктер
Qatıstı etistikter

to bring

әкелу

äkelu

to cough

жөтелу

jötelu

to examine

тексеру

tekseru

to explain

түсіндіру

tüsindiru

to feel

сезу

sezu

to give

беру

beru

to hurt

ауырту

auırtu

to prescribe

дәріқағаз беру

däriqağaz beru

---

to scan

қарау

qarau

---

to take

алу

alu

---

to test

тексеру

tekseru

---

to treat

емдеу

emdeu

---

to visit

келу

kelu

---

to wait

күту

kütu

---

to x-ray

рентгенге түсіру

rentgenge tüsiru

James was a happy, **healthy** ten year old boy who loved sports and riding his bike; but one day that all came to a halt. James had been complaining that his back was hurting. The **pain** was so bad one morning; he couldn't even get out of bed. His mom decided to take him to the **emergency room** to get **examined** by a **doctor**. The **nurses** were very friendly and their number one priority was making sure James was not in **pain** and could rest comfortably. The **doctor** decided to order an **x-ray** of his back. The **radiologist** read the report; he and the **ER doctor** agreed that James had an unknown **mass** on his spine. James was immediately admitted to the **hospital** for **blood tests**. The **blood tests** did not reveal the cause of the **mass,** so the **pediatrician** overseeing his **case** decided he needed some more extensive **imaging tests**, as well as a **biopsy**. James was nervous because so many **doctors** were coming to see him; an **orthopedic doctor**, a **neurosurgeon,** and a **hematologist.** The **nurses** did a good job at keeping his mind at ease. They brought him movies and video games to play to keep him busy. He had many **visitors**; friends and family members came to see him. He loved the visits with the **therapy** dogs the most; they were such comforting and sweet dogs. They had so many activities and fun for the **patients** at the children's **hospital.** James was a real trooper when they had to take **blood** and put his **IV** in his arm. James spent twelve days in the **hospital** before they finally **diagnosed** him with a **bone infection**. The **physical therapist** fit him with a back brace and he was **prescribed antibiotics**. After undergoing multiple **blood tests, image scans**, and a **biopsy**, James was ready to go home. He was not able to do the normal things other kids could do because of the damage to his spine, but he was so happy to be home with his family and on the mend from his terrible back

infection. After several months of **treatment** and spinal **surgery** to straighten his back, James is now a strong, healthy, and happy boy. Through it all; the t**reatments, tests, hospital** stays, and **therapy**, James has been an inspiration and hero to many who walked this journey with him.

Джеймс спортты және велосипед айдағанды ұнататын бақытты он жасар **дені сау** бала. Бірақ бір күні бұның барлығы өзгерді. Джеймс арқасының ауыратынын айтты. Бір күні таңертең оның арқасының ауырғаны сонша, ол кереуетінен тұра алмай қалды. Оның анасы оны **дәрігерге тексерту** үшін **шапшаң жәрдем ету бөліміне** алып келуді шешті. **Медбикелер** жылы шырайлы болды және олар Джеймстің өзін жайлы сезінуі және **ауыруын** басуы олар үшін ең бастысы болды. **Дәрігер** оның арқасын **рентгенге** түсіруге тапсырыс берді. **Радиолог** жазбаны оқыды; ол және ШЖ **дәрігері** оның омыртқасында белгісіз бір **масса** бар екен деп шешті. Джеймске **ауруханада қан тексеру**і рұқсат етілді. **Қан талдауы массаның** шығу себебін анықтамаған соң, **педиатр** оның **жағдайын** қарап шығып, оған **биопсия** секілді **бейнелеу тексерісі** қажет деп шешті. Джеймс мазасыздана бастады, өйткені **ортопедиялық дәрігер, нейрохирург** және **гематолог** және тағы басқа көп дәрігерлер оны қарап шықты. Оның көңілін аулау үшін **медбикелер** жақсы қызмет атқарды, оның қолы босамас үшін олар оған фильмдер мен видео ойындар әкеліп берді. Оның көптеген **келушілері** болды. Достары мен жанұя мүшелері оны көруге келіп тұратын. Ол **терапиялық** иттердің келгенін ұнататын. Олар сондай жайлы және сүйкімді иттер. Балалар **ауруханасындағы емделушілерді** қызықтыратын сонша көп алданыштар бар. Қолындағы **көктамырдан қан** алу кезінде Джеймс нағыз сарбаз болды. Нәтижесінде **сүйек инфекциясы диагнозын** қойғанша, Джеймс **ауруханада** он екі күн жатты. **Терапевт** арқасына **қапсырма** бекітіп, **антибиотиктер** жазып берді. Көптеген қан **талдауларынан**, **бейнелеу тексерістерінен** және **биопсиядан** кейін ол үйіне баруға дайын болды. Ол омыртқасының зақымдалуынан басқа балалардай қарапайым қимылдарды атқара алмайтын, бірақ ол жанұясының ортасына үйіне келгеніне және жаман арқа инфекциясынан емделгеніне бақытты болды. **Емделудің** бірнеше айларынан және арқасын түзейтін омыртқа **операциясынан** кейін Джеймс енді мықты, дені сау және бақытты бала. Осының бәрінен; **емшаралардан**, **тексерістерден, ауруханадан** жатудан, және **терапиядан** өткен Джеймс онымен бірге осы жолдан өткен адамдарға шабыт беріп, батыр болды.

Jeyms sporttı jäne velosïped aydağandı unatatın on jasar **deni sau** baqıttı bala. Biraq bir küni bunıñ barlığı özgerdi. Jeyms arqasınıñ auıratının ayttı. Bir küni tañerteñ onıñ arqasınıñ auırğanı sonşa, ol kereuetinen tura almay qaldı. Onıñ anası onı **därigerge teksertu** üşin **şapşañ järdem etu bölimine** alıp keludi şeşti. **Medbïkeler** jılı şıraylı boldı jäne olar Jeymstın özin jaylı sezinui jäne **auıruın** basuı olar üşin eñ bastısı boldı.. **Däriger** onıñ arqasın **rentgenge** tüsiruge tapsırıs berdi. **Radïolog** jazbanı oqıdı; ol jäne ŞJ **därigeri** onıñ omırtqasında belgisiz bir **massa** bar eken dep şeşti. Jeymske **auruxanada qan tekserui** ruqsat etildi. **Qan taldauı** massanıñ şığu sebebin anıqtamağan soñ, **pedïatr** onıñ **jağdayın** qarap şığıp, oğan **bïopsïya** sekildi **beyneleu tekserisi** qajet dep şeşti. Jeyms mazasızdana bastadı, öytkeni **ortopedïyalıq däriger**, **neyroxïrurg** jäne **gematolog** jäne tağı basqa köp därigerler onı qarap şıqtı. Onıñ köñilin aulau üşin **medbïkeler** jaqsı qızmet atqardı, onıñ qolı bosamas üşin olar oğan fil'mder men vïdeo oyındar äkelip berdi. Onıñ köptegen **keluşileri** boldı. Dostarı men januya müşeleri onı köruge kelip turatın. Ol **terapïyalıq** ïtterdiñ kelgenin unatatın. Olar sonday jaylı jäne süykimdi ïtter. Balalar **auruxanasındağı emdeluşilerdi** qızıqtıratın sonşa köp aldanıştar bar. Qolındağı **köktamırdan qan** alu kezinde Jeyms nağız sarbaz boldı. Nätïjesinde **süyek ïnfekcïyası dïagnozın** qoyğanşa, Djeyms **auruxanada** on eki kün jattı. **Terapevt** arqasına **qapsırma** bekitip, **antïbïotïkter** jazıp berdi. Köptegen qan **taldaularınan, beyneleu tekseristerinen** jäne **bïopsïyadan** keyin ol üyine baruğa dayın boldı. Ol omırtqasınıñ zaqımdaluınan basqa balalarday qarapayım qïmıldardı atqara almaytın, biraq ol januyasınıñ ortasına üyine kelgenine jäne jaman arqa ïnfekcïyasınan emdelgenine baqıttı boldı. **Emdeludiñ** birneşe aylarınan jäne arqasın tüzeytin omırtqa **operacïyasınan** keyin Jeyms endi mıqtı, deni sau jäne baqıttı bala. Osınıñ bärinen; **emşaralardan, tekseristerden, auruxanadan** jatudan, jäne **terapïyadan** ötken Jeyms onımen birge osı joldan ötken adamdarğa şabıt şabıt berip, batır boldı.

18) Emergency
18) Төтенше жағдай
18) Tötenşe jağday

accident

апат

apat

---

aftershock

соққы

soqqı

---

ambulance

жедел жәрдем көлігі

jedel järdem köligi

---

asthma attack

демікпе ұстау

demikpe ustau

---

avalanche

көшкін

köşkin

---

blizzard

боран

boran

---

blood/bleeding

қан/қан ағу

qan/qan ağu

broken bone

сынған сүйек

sınğan süyek

car accident

көлік апаты

kölik apatı

chest pain

кеуде ауыруы

keude auıruı

choking

тұншығу

tunşığu

coast guard

жағажай күзеті

jağajay küzeti

crash

соқтығыс

soqtığıs

diabetes

сусамыр

susamır

doctor

дәрігер

däriger

drought

құрғақшылық

qurğaqşılıq

drowning

су тасқыны

su tasqını

earthquake

жер сілкінісі

jer silkinisi

emergency

төтенше жағдай

tötenşe jağday

emergency services

апаттан құтқару қызметі

apattan qutqaru qızmeti

EMT (emergency medical technician)

медициналық жедел жәрдем техникасының маманы

medïcïnalıq jedel järdem texnïkasınıñ mamanı

explosion

жарылыс

jarılıs

fight

төбелес

töbeles

---

fire

өрт

ört

---

fire department

өрт сөндірушілер бөлімі

ört söndiruşiler bölimi

---

fire escape

өрт баспалдағы

ört baspaldağı

---

firefighter

өрт сөндіруші

ört söndiruşi

---

fire truck

өрт сөндіру көлігі

ört söndiru köligi

---

first aid

алғашқы көмек

alğaşqı kömek

---

flood

су тасқыны

su tasqını

---

fog

тұман

tuman

gun

қару

qaru

gunshot

атыс

atıs

heart attack

жүрек ұстау

jürek ustau

heimlich maneuver

жасырын манёвр

jasırın manyovr

help

көмек

kömek

hospital

аурухана

auruxana

hurricane

дауыл

dauıl

injury

жарақат

jaraqat

---

ladder

баспалдақ

baspaldaq

---

lifeguard

құтқарушы

qutqaruşı

---

life support

тіршілікті қамтамасыз ету

tirşilikti qamtamasız etu

---

lightening

жарықтандыру

jarıqtandıru

---

lost

жоғалған

joğalğan

---

mudslide

көшкін

köşkin

---

natural disaster

табиғи апат

tabïğï apat

---

nurse

медбике

medbïke

---

officer

офицер

oficer

---

paramedic

медициналық қызметкер

medïcïnalıq qızmetker

---

poison

у

u

---

police

полиция қызметкері

polïcïya qızmetkeri

---

police car

полиция көлігі

polïcïya köligi

---

rescue

құтқару

qutqaru

---

robbery

ұрлық

urlıq

---

shooting

атыс

atıs

---

stop

тоқтау

toqtau

---

storm

дауыл

dauıl

---

stroke

соққы

soqqı

---

temperature

температура

temperatura

---

thief

ұры

urı

---

tornado

торнадо

tornado

---

tsunami

цунами

cunamï

---

unconscious

ессіз

essiz

---

weather emergency

ауа райылық төтенше жағдайы

awa rayılıq tötenşe jağdayı

Related Verbs
Қатысты етістіктер

Qatıstı etistikter

---

to bleed

қан ағу

qan ağu

---

to break

сындыру

sındıru

---

to breathe

тыныс алу

tınıs alu

---

to call

қоңырау шалу

qoñırau şalu

---

to crash

соқтығысу

soqtığısu

---

to cut

қысқарту

qısqartu

---

to burn

өртену

örtenu

---

to escape

шығу

şığu

---

to faint

әлсіреу

älsireu

---

to fall

құлау

qulau

---

to help

көмектесу

kömektesu

---

to hurt

ауырту

auırtu

---

to rescue

құтқару

qutqaru

---

to save

құтқару

qutqaru

---

to shoot

ату

atu

---

to wheeze

ентігу

entigu

---

to wreck

бұзу

buzu

One of the most important things parents can teach their children is how to handle an **emergency**. You often hear stories on the news about a child who saved someone by making a wise decision in an **emergency**. What you don't hear are the stories when children made a poor decision. Unfortunately, many children would not know what to do in case of a real **emergency** such as a **fire**, a **flood**, or if a parent had a **heart attack**. We hope that our children are never put in these situations, but we want them to be prepared. In an **emergency**, such as a **tornado**, an **earthquake**, or other **natural disaster,** children might react in two very dangerous ways; one of which is the superhero reaction. In this case, children think they can "save the day" and play **rescue** worker. They might try to run into a burning building or swim out to save someone in a **flood.** Make sure your children know that there are people such as **firefighters**, **police officers**, and **EMTs** that are professionally trained to handle these situations. It may seem safe to "**help**", but the danger may not be obvious to a child. If they try to "**help**" in a dangerous situation, it may make the **emergency** worse! The best thing to do is call **emergency services** and they will tell you exactly what you can do to **help**. On the other hand, the opposite reaction can be just as dangerous. Some children will try to run and hide from scary situations. Even though you may be scared, try to remain calm, find a phone, and call for **help**. As I said earlier, children often play a big role in the **rescue** efforts during an **emergency**. Here are some practical tips to teach your children about **emergency** situations. 1) Take a deep breath, relax and look around for **help**. 2) Call for **help**; either by yelling or phone. If someone has an **injury** or are hurt, the **rescue** workers can be there fast. In a **life threatening** situation, the **emergency operator** can often walk you through step-by-step what to do. 3) Never hang up on the operator; they will need details about your location and the **emergency** situation. 4) Find a safe place to wait for help. Do not put yourself in danger while you wait for the professionals, it will only create a bigger **emergency**. The best way to handle an **emergency** is to prepare yourself for one. If you know what to do in different **emergencies**, you will be better equipped to handle them. Ask your parents to teach you the **fire escape** plan in your home or what to do in case someone is **injured** at home. Ask someone to show you how to call for help; make sure the phone numbers for the **fire department**, **police**, and **ambulance** service numbers are posted on your home phone. As you get older, you can even take a **first aid** class. Remember, in all **emergencies**, remain calm and call for help and never put yourself in danger.

Ата-аналардың балаларына үйрете алатын ең маңызды зат ол **төтенше жағдайда** қалай әрекет ету. Біздер жаңалықтардан қалай баланың **төтенше жағдай** кезінде дұрыс шешім қабылдау арқылы біреуді құтқарғаны туралы жиі естиміз. Неге сіз балалардың бұрыс шешім қабылдағаны туралы әңгімелерді естімейсіз. Негізінде көп балалар **өрт**, **су тасқыны** немесе ата-ананың **жүрек ұстауы** секілді шынайы **төтенше жағдай** кезінде не істеу керек екендігін білмейді. Біздің балаларымыз мұндай жағдайға ешқашан тап болмайды деп сенеміз, алайда біз олардың дайын болғанын қалаймыз. **Торнадо, жер сілкінісі** немесе басқа **табиғи апаттары** секілді **төтенше жағдай** кезінде балалар екі қауіпті шешім қабылдауы мүмкін; олардың бірі бұл супер қаһарман реакциясы. Бұл жағдайда балалар "күнді құтқара аламыз" деп ойлап, **құтқару** қызметшісі болып ойнауы мүмкін. Олар біреуді құтқарамыз деп өртеніп жатқан ғимарат ішіне кіруге немесе **су тасқыны** кезінде суға жүзуге ұмтылуы мүмкін. Балаларыңыздың мұндай жағдайда қалай әрекет ету керектігін білетін кәсіби жаттыққан **өрт сөндірушілер, полиция офицерлері** және **медициналық жедел жәрдем техникасының маманы** бар екендігін білетініне куә болыңыз. "**Көмектесу**" қауіпсіз болып көріну мүмкін, алайда қауіпті бала байқамауы да мүмкін. Егер олар қауіпті жағдайда "**көмектесуге**" тырысса, олар **қауіпті жағдайды** одан бетер нашарлатуы мүмкін. Ең дұрысы құтқару қызметін шақыру және олар сізге нақты сол жағдайда **көмектесу** үшін не істеу керектігін айтады. Басқа жағынан, қарсы реакция да солай қауіпті болуы мүмкін. Кейбір балалар қорқынышты жағдайдан қашуға немесе тығылуға тырысады. Қорыққан жағдайда да, сабырлық сақтауға тырысыңыз, телефонды тауып, **көмек** сұрауға қоңырау шалыңыз. Мен бұрын айтқандай, **төтенше жағдай** кезіндегі **құтқару** әсеріне балалар жиі маңызды рөл атқарады. Мұнда балаларыңызға **төтенше жағдай** туралы үйретудің пайдалы кейбір кеңестер бар. 1) Терең дем алыңыз, босаңсып, **көмек** сұрау үшін айналаңа қараңыз. 2) **Көмекке** шақырыңыз: айқайлау немесе телефон арқылы. Егер біреу **жарақат алса** немесе бір жерін ауыртып алса, **құтқарушылар** тез арада келеді. **Өмірге қауіпті** жағдайда **төтенше жағдай операторы** не істеу керек екендігін түсіндіреді. 3) Ешқашан оператормен байланысты үзбеңіз, оған сіздің тұрған мекенжайыңыз бен **төтенше жағдайыңыз** туралы білуі керек. 4) Көмекті күту үшін қауіпсіз жерді табыңыз. Кәсіби мамандар келгенше, өзіңізді қауіпке ұшыратпаңыз, өйткені сіз **төтенше жағдайды** одан бетер ушықтырып жіберуіңіз мүмкін. **Төтенше жағдайды** қолға алудың ең дұрыс жолы –оған дайын болу. Егер сіз түрлі **төтенше жағдайлар** кезіне дайын болсаңыз, оларды қолға алуда сіз көбірек қамтамалы боласыз. Ата-аналарыңыздан үйді **өрттен эвакуациялау** жоспарын немесе үйде біреу **жарақат** алған жағдайда не істеу керектігін үйретуін сұраңыз. Біреуден көмек шақыруға қоңырау шалуды үйретуін сұраңыз. **Өрт сөндіру**, **полиция** және **аурухана** қызметтерінің нөмірлері сіздің телефоныңызға енгізілгеніне куә болыңыз. Ересек болғанда, сіз **алғашқы көмек** сыныбына баруыңызға болады. Есте сақтаңыз, барлық **төтенше жағдай** кезінде сабырлық сақтаңыз және көмек шақырыңыз және ешқашан өзіңізді қауіпке төндірмеңіз.

Ata-analardıñ balalarına üyrete alatın eñ mañızdı zat ol **tötenşe jağdayda** qalay äreket etu. Bizder jañalıqtardan qalay balanıñ **tötenşe jağday** kezinde durıs şeşim qabıldau arqılı bireudi qutqarğanı twralı jii estimiz. Nege siz balalardıñ burıs şeşim qabıldağanı turalı äñgimelerdi estimeysiz. Negizinde köp balalar **ört, su tasqını** nemese ata-ananıñ **jürek ustauı** sekildi şınayı **tötenşe jağday** kezinde ne isteu kerek ekendigin bilmeydi. Bizdiñ balalarımız munday jağdayğa eşqaşan tap bolmaydı dep senemiz, alayda biz olardıñ dayın bolğanın qalaymız. **Tornado, jer silkinisi** nemese basqa **tabiğı apattarı** sekildi **tötenşe jağday** kezinde balalar eki qauipti şeşim qabıldauı mümkin; olardıñ biri bul super qaharman reakciyası. Bul jağdayda balalar "kündi qutqara alamız" dep oylap, **qutqaru** qızmetşisi bolıp oynauı mümkin. Olar bireudi qutqaramız dep örtenip jatqan ğimarat işine kiruge nemese **su tasqını** kezinde suğa jüzuge umtıluı mümkin. Balalarıñızdıñ munday jağdayda qalay äreket etu kerektigin biletin käsibï jattıqqan **ört söndiruşiler, policïya oficerleri** jäne **medïcïnalıq jedel järdem texnïkasınıñ mamanı** bar ekendigin biletinine kuä bolıñız. "Kömektesu" qauipsiz bolıp körinu mümkin, alayda qauipti bala bayqamayuı da mümkin. Eger olar qauipti jağdayda "**kömektesuge**" tırıssa, olar **qauipti jağdaydı** odan beter naşarlatuı mümkin. Eñ durısı qutqaru qızmetin şaqıru jäne olar sizge naqtı sol jağdayda **kömektesu** üşin ne isteu kerektigin aytadı. Basqa jağınan, qarsı reakciya da solay qauipti boluı mümkin. Keybir balalar qorqınıştı jağdaydan qaşuğa nemese tığıluğa tırısadı. Qorıqqan jağdayda da, sabırlıq saqtauğa tırısıñız, telefondı tauıp, **kömek** surauğa qoñırau şalıñız. Men burın aytqanday, **tötenşe jağday** kezindegi **qutqaru** äserine balalar jii mañızdı röl atqaradı. Munda balalarıñızğa **tötenşe jağday** turalı üyretudiñ paydalı keybir keñesteri bar. 1) Tereñ dem alıñız, bosañsyp, **kömek** surau üşin aynalaña qarañız. 2) **Kömekke** şaqırıñız: ayqaylau nemese telefon arqılı. Eger bireu **jaraqat alsa** nemese bir jerin auırtıp alsa, **qutqaruşılar** tez arada keledi. **Ömirge qauipti** jağdayda **tötenşe jağday operatorı** ne isteu kerek ekendigin tüsindiredi. 3) Eşqaşan **operatormen** baylanıs üzbeñiz, oğan sizdiñ turğan mekenjayıñız ben **tötenşe jağdayıñız** turalı bilui kerek. 4) Kömekti kütu üşin qauipsiz jerdi tabıñız. Käsibï mamandar kelgenşe, öziñizdi qauipke uşıratpañız, öytkeni siz **tötenşe jağdaydı** odan beter uşıqtırıp jiberuiñiz mümkin. **Tötenşe jağdaydı** qolğa aludıñ eñ durıs jolı –oğan dayın bolu. Eger siz türli **tötenşe jağdaylar** kezine dayın bolsañız, olardı qolğa aluda siz köbirek qamtamalı bolasız. Ata-analarıñızdan üydi **örtten évakuacïyalau** josparın nemese üyde bireu **jaraqat** alğan jağdayda ne isteu kerektigin üyretuin surañız. Bireuden kömek şaqıruğa qoñırau şaludı üyretuin surañız. **Ört söndiru**, **polïcïya** jäne **auruxana** qızmetteriniñ nömirleri sizdiñ telefonıñızğa engizilgenine kuä bolıñız. Eresek bolğanda, siz **alğaşqı kömek** sınıbına baruıñızğa boladı. Este saqtañız, barlıq **tötenşe jağday** kezinde sabırlıq saqtañız jäne kömek şaqırıñız jäne eşqaşan öziñizdi qauipke töndirmeñiz.

www.ingramcontent.com/pod-product-compliance
Lightning Source LLC
Chambersburg PA
CBHW051938090426
42741CB00008B/1187